MW00715467

"Restore the honeymoon . . .

"The minute I saw Pamala Kennedy at one of our C.L.A.S.S. seminars, I knew that she had something special. She had an energy and a passion for life that I seldom see. As I got to know Pam, I discovered her secret. The central relationship in her life was strong and healthy. Pam and her husband are 'lovers.' Through *Where Have All the Lovers Gone?* you will learn to capture a new joy for life and restore the honeymoon to your marriage."

Florence Littauer
Author, *Make the Tough Times Count*

"I have never seen two unselfish people get a divorce. People who really love each other can hold any relationship together. Pamala Kennedy has given us a book that encourages and strengthens the love relationship between husbands and wives."

Bob Phillips, Ph.D.
Licensed Marriage, Family
and Child Counselor

"When I first met Pamala Kennedy I was instantly impressed by her beauty, her discernment, and her enthusiasm. In *Where Have All the Lovers Gone?* Pam provides practical ways to make even the best marriages better. Women of all ages will benefit from the wealth of wisdom offered in this book."

Marilyn Willett Heavilin
Author, *When Your Dreams Die*

Where Have All the *Lovers* Gone?

Pamala Condit Kennedy

Here's Life Publishers

First Printing, July 1990

Published by
HERE'S LIFE PUBLISHERS, INC.
P. O. Box 1576
San Bernardino, CA 92402

Library of Congress Cataloging-in-Publication Data
Kennedy, Pamala Condit.
    Where have all the lovers gone? : becoming your husband's
favorite person / Pamala Condit Kennedy.
        p.   cm.
    Includes bibliographical references.
    ISBN 0-89840-292-1
    1. Marriage — United States. 2. Interpersonal relations.
  3. Intimacy (Psychology) I. Title.
    HQ734.K3815   1990
    306.81 — dc 20   90-33884
                                    CIP

Cover design by Michelle Treiber. Photographed at The Palisades, Moreno Valley, California and used by permission of Inland Pacific Communities, Inc.

Unless otherwise designated, Scripture quotations are from *The Holy Bible: New International Version,* © 1973, 1978, 1984 by the International Bible Society. Used by permission of Zondervan Bible Publishers.
    Scripture quotations designated NASB are from *The New American Standard Bible,* © The Lockman Foundation 1960, 1962, 1963, 1968, 1971, 1972, 1975, 1977.
    Scripture quotations designated KJV are from the *King James Version.*

For More Information, Write:
L.I.F.E. — P.O. Box A399, Sydney South 2000, Australia
Campus Crusade for Christ of Canada — Box 300, Vancouver, B.C., V6C 2X3, Canada
Campus Crusade for Christ — Pearl Assurance House, 4 Temple Row, Birmingham, B2 5HG, England
Lay Institute for Evangelism — P.O. Box 8786, Auckland 3, New Zealand
Campus Crusade for Christ — P.O. Box 240, Raffles City Post Office, Singapore 9117
Great Commission Movement of Nigeria — P.O. Box 500, Jos, Plateau State Nigeria, West Africa
Campus Crusade for Christ International — Arrowhead Springs, San Bernardino, CA 92414, U.S.A.

To Richard,
my husband,
lover,
best friend
and encourager.

Thank you for believing in me
and choosing me to be yours.

*Where has your lover gone,
most beautiful of women?
Which way did your lover turn,
that we may look for him with you?*

Song of Solomon 6:1

Contents

Foreword

Solomon said, "He who finds a wife finds a good thing, and obtains favor from the LORD" (Proverbs 18:22, NASB). I'll second that motion! It is truly amazing how God, through circumstance and providence, brings two people together and makes them "one flesh"; most often two very different people. Such is our case.

The pages that follow come from the heart and soul of the one I love. She is one woman who loves her God and her husband. I have learned so much from Pam about loving and being loved. She writes from her twenty years of marriage, nineteen years as being a pastor's wife, and many years as being a faithful friend.

Having been born a PK (pastor's kid), Pam should have known better than to marry a pastor! Yet in the midst of all the demands of ministry, she has taken time to be a faithful friend, a loving wife and a godly mother.

The pages that follow will be both challenging and stretching. The personal challenge at the end of each chapter will hold you accountable for what you've read.

Go ahead . . . I dare you. The call to intimacy involves risk, transparency and vulnerability. But the dividends are well worth the investment.

Richard P. Kennedy
(One Very Happy Husband)

*Is romancing him
as important to you now
as when you were "just married"?*

O · N · E

"Everybody Loves Somebody— Sometimes"?

*D*o you remember when loving that special someone was on your mind continually? He was your first thought each morning and the last thought as you drifted off to sleep. You actually began on Monday deciding what to wear to the football game on Friday because *he* was going to be there. Remember keeping everyone off the phone (this was in the days when teenagers didn't have private lines of their own) because he just might call?

We made certain not to get caught in hair rollers or without makeup. It is not so different with teenage girls today. Before my daughter leaves for a date, she has tried on every outfit twice and asked the entire household if this one makes her look fat or skinny.

We all, at one time or another, lived for the moment

to be with that special someone. The evening would fly by so fast. Curfew was never late enough. Being apart was worse than having the flu! No appetite, rather desperate and sick all over . . . love sick! The excitement and anticipation of being together created more energy than Niagara Falls. Then he finally asked the big question, you gave the big "Yes" and the planning of a royal wedding began.

So much time, a vast amount of energy and, as dads will all agree, far too much money is spent on a ceremony which will last about forty minutes, tops! But it is breathtakingly beautiful and the memories are worth the time and money. All of this to join two lives, to merge two into one. And so it all begins, because of love.

Because of love, we want to build something together. We work to buy our first home. Then come furniture and all the trimmings. So begins the job, the house, the furniture, the car, and the payments. We started all of this because of love. It is a beautiful dream . . . a lovely house with a lovely yard, a driveway with a lovely car, lovely children playing joyfully while mom and dad smile and chat with the friendly neighbors. The very substance which holds this picture together is that special feeling that was kindled in the beginning—*love.*

All of these lovely things take time, lots of time. So much time is spent on the *things* of life that through the years we may forget to keep love nurtured and tenderly cared for. Anything left uncared for will soon show signs of neglect.

A few years ago my four-year-old son gave me an elegant African violet for Valentine's Day. This violet was laden with delicate blooms. I enjoyed their beauty for days. Then one by one they turned brown and shriveled up like dried apricots. I got busy with other tasks and soon even the leaves were wilting. I gave the plant some water and promptly forgot about it. Thus began the lifestyle of this poor violet. Only when I noticed it was drooping would I water it. This regular ritual continued for several years. I managed to keep it alive . . . but that was all. I gave it no real care, just the bare minimum needed for survival.

A few weeks ago I saw some lovely violets in full bloom and I really wanted to purchase one. Immediately I thought of the poor neglected plant in my kitchen. Feeling very convicted, I bought fertilizer instead of a new plant. That evening I made a commitment to my violet. I watered, trimmed and fertilized it. Within days I had the most lavish African violet in town. Its beauty had been waiting to burst out. I was holding that beauty back. I had been denying myself the opportunity of seeing that beauty each day for the past several years . . . because of neglect.

Every marriage has within it the possibility of being a gorgeous masterpiece, something of great beauty deep within. But abuse, neglect, or even doing just the bare minimum of maintenance, keeps married love from blossoming into the radiant flower it can be.

Take Time Now

We give time to everyone and everything else for years and then wonder where the love has gone. What will happen when the children are grown and busy enjoying their own lives? What will you do when friends have moved away or moved on without you? What will you be left with if you face retirement much sooner than expected? Just the TV, the dog, and a stranger who looks vaguely familiar?

It disturbs me to see my friends, after investing twenty-five to thirty years, break up their marriages. This is when they should be enjoying the ecstasy years. They have more financial security and freedom from the responsibility of raising children. They have more time to spend together, uninterrupted time for each other. Unfortunately, this is very frightening for couples who haven't spent time working on their personal intimacy through the years.

My good friend Kathy went through this experience. After twenty-five years of mothering, her occupation ended abruptly as the last of her little chicks left the nest. She described this new experience as "the very depths of despair. I felt the main part of my life was finished. I was terrified of the future."

As she spoke, I could feel the pain she suffered. She explained, "I knew it was coming the year our son Tim—the last to leave the nest—was to be married. I read all the books I could get my hands on about rekindling the love we had as newlyweds." She chuckled a bit as she admitted putting these books under her husband's nose each morning during breakfast so he, too, would be ready for this moment. But they found themselves unready.

Following the wedding they arrived home exhausted. Jim parked the car, they walked up the sidewalk to the house and he opened the front door. Kathy said, "I stood frozen in the doorway, unable to move as I looked into a big, quiet, empty nest!" When they went into their bedroom that night and turned off the light, the loneliness swallowed them up. She thought, *My life is over!* She prayed, "Lord, if you don't make this awful pain go away I want to die this very night." Even though she and Jim lay side by side, they were strangers.

Kathy agonized over their failure through the years to stay tuned in to each other. Looking back, she regretted they hadn't taken quiet walks together or had more romantic meals alone. For years they both had hidden behind the hollering and hustle of children and the slavery of a work schedule. Kathy and Jim finally had to admit, "We do not enjoy being left alone with each other." It was worse than facing a stranger. At least a stranger doesn't know the dreadful faults and weaknesses that have developed over the years.

Kathy and Jim are presently working hard to rekindle their relationship. They know their marriage is worth saving. However, many married couples are opting to throw their marriages away and start over, which inevitably brings more pain and sadness than they bargained for.

In physical illnesses, doctors most readily agree that prevention is far less painful than having to go through treatment. With the dentist, brushing and flossing daily is a piece of cake compared to the pain of drilling, filling and capping. Cleaning the house regularly is far easier than sending in the bulldozer to face a mountain of grime once a year.

What am I saying? Take time now! Take the time to be a lover to your husband. Don't allow the urgent things in life to keep you from attending to the important.

Perhaps you need to do what I did this year. When I realized I was getting so busy that my time with Richard suffered, I made a list of all outside things I was involved in. I crossed off those I did not thoroughly enjoy. I set up ground rules and determined to stick to them. We have set aside a family night and nothing or nobody can have that night except our family. My husband and I have a date night that is exclusively ours. I chose one night for extracurricular activities and one night for ministry.

Since we attend Sunday night services as well, we are left with only two "flex" nights just to be home or with friends or at ball games or whatever. I do housework one day each week and laundry one day (all day) each week, with one evening for catch-up loads. If I am with friends or have meetings, parties or appointments, it must be when the kids are in school and my husband is at work.

Not everyone has the freedom to set up their schedule as I did. You will have to make your own rules and shape them around your work schedule and your family's needs. But please, do not waste precious time on just being busy, spinning wheels that go nowhere. Make time your friend. Take time for love. Don't let it fade or wilt. Cherish it, nurture it, protect it.

Has your love grown weary from you working day and night? Has it been neglected because of wasting time? Or is it out of balance because you are constantly with the kids? Bring your relationship priorities back into focus. Do you really want him as you did way back when? Remember, your husband needs love—and more than just sometimes.

T · W · O

Are Your Priorities "All Shook Up"?

Let's face it. Even when our intentions are good, it's not easy being wife, lover, confidante, mother, career woman, volunteer worker, home administrator and cab driver.

Much as we would like to take more time to fan the romantic flames of our marriages, there is only so much time in the day — and only so much energy in the woman.

So let's begin with an honest look at three subtle, yet common, time-and-energy consumers that often hinder marital intimacy. If we can get these under control, we can re-discover the time and energy to actually implement the ideas in this book.

Wasting Time

Most homes just a generation ago had only a newspaper, radio, Bible and maybe a literary classic for reading aloud. How do we spend leisure time in the 1990s? We find in the average home at least one color remote-control TV, a stereo, a VCR, many books, radios of all shapes and sizes, two telephones, comic books, cassette recorders, video games, table games, tons of sporting equipment, and maybe a spa or swimming pool. The list of entertainment goes on and on. More and more things fight for our time and attention.

An American household has the TV set on an average of about seven hours a day.[2] The national media reports married couples spend 70 percent of their leisure time watching TV while only 11 percent of that time is given to intimacy. Isn't it time to turn off the TV and turn on to each other?

This might sound painfully familiar. One man sprawled himself on the sofa and flipped through the channels with the remote control. Finding nothing to his liking, he turned desperately to his wife and said, "Sandy, there's nothing on TV tonight. Run down and rent a video."

I'm not against TV or renting an entertaining movie. Cuddled on the couch watching a movie together can be part of a relaxing evening. The problem occurs when the TV replaces the time we need with each other for communication and play. We are too dependent on the TV to fill our spare moments. Be brave. Turn off the TV and share a mellow cup of coffee and some quiet conversation. Go for a walk. Put on some soft, slow music and hold each other close. Plan a date, talk about the future, dream together. Do not waste precious time.

Friends Who Want Too Much

Friends who dominate our private time together can also be considered a waste of time. Friends who want to spend hours on the phone or occupy three or four nights a week are wasting quality time we could be spending with our spouse. Watch out for these friends.

I know couples who always seem to be with other people. It is as if they cannot stand to be alone with each other. They take friends along on evenings out and even vacation with other couples.

Don't let well-meaning friends—men or women—rob you of your precious time together. Your intimacy as husband and wife needs privacy.

Too much time spent with another couple could also prove dangerous. One author warns: "Loose sex-talk breaks down the protective walls, stirs up the curiosity and encourages fantasies. The more open and transparent the friendship, the more necessary to keep conversation on a high level."[3] How tragic to hear the news of marriages breaking up because of a friendship romance.

As a pastor's wife I see this happen far too often in the church family. There is a natural closeness found in the body of Christ. We bare our very souls and share openly. This intimacy of spirit tends to break down natural walls and can result in an attraction toward friends of the opposite sex.

When we are intimate spiritually and share a close heart-to-heart friendship, we dare not be close physically as well. Be careful of friends who want to touch, hug or always have their hands on you. A bad situation can develop from an innocent gesture.

Steve was a young pastor, Jill a brand-new bride. They moved to the West Coast for a great new life together. This was Steve's first pastorate and he certainly had capacious dreams for their new ministry there. This small church, tucked away amidst the green trees of Washington, was a tremendous challenge to the newly-graduated minister. He had plans to evangelize the entire city. He began his work as soon as the last box was carried into the small, two-bedroom house.

Steve's every thought and action centered around the challenge of building that small church into something colossal. The congregation had a building, but it needed paint, pews and people. So the work began. By day, Steve worked on the building and at night he concentrated on meeting new people. It was on one of those cool, rainy nights that Steve met Dick. Dick was a few years his senior, and a few thousand dollars more well-to-do, but they became fast friends.

Sarah, Dick's wife, was the mothering type who took to shy, lovely Jill right away. Sarah and Dick became family for the young couple; the four friends spent much time together, both at church social happenings and quietly in each others' homes. They shared happy and sad stories, spiritual victories and secret sins. They were the best of friends.

Then one night when they went out to dinner together, Jill noticed a change in Dick's attentiveness toward her. He managed to touch Jill's arm or hand several times throughout the evening. The touch was not like the times before when they would greet or say good night. Now Dick's touch was tender, warm, lingering. *What was this change all about?* thought Jill as she lay sleepless throughout the night.

The following morning her questions were answered as Dick stood at her front door, heart in hand. "Jill, I am so sorry, so ashamed to tell you this, but I cannot keep silent any longer. I find myself helplessly in love with you! I think of you constantly. Steve has no idea what a prize he has in you. If you were my wife, I'd keep you by my side all day just delighting in your beauty."

Dick was appealing to Jill's loneliness and very neglected romantic nature. She knew it was a sin, a scheme from Satan, forbidden fruit, but she could not slam the door in his face—she enjoyed the flattery. Steve had been so preoccupied with the church the past several months, completely ignoring her.

"All I wanted from Dick was companionship," Jill told me later. She rationalized to herself that they could be close friends, enjoy long conversations on the phone, and never hurt anyone. But soon the calls were not enough. They met secretly—just to talk, of course. The talking led to touching, and the line Jill had drawn in the beginning kept moving. The friendship became a hot, passionate sexual relationship. Since neither Dick nor Jill could live with the guilt and lies, they fled together in the night, leaving unsuspecting Steve and Sarah sleeping soundly in their deserted homes.

Dick and Jill married, but it was a marriage built on lies, deceit and guilt. The little church Steve desired to build up was destroyed by gossip. He was forced to turn in his much-loved ordination papers and sell insurance. Sarah totally flipped out, and to this day lives on prescription drugs. Four intimate friends, who all wish now they had never met.

Close friendship with the opposite sex does not always mean an affair is imminent, but the closer the friendship, the greater the odds that sex could become a part of it. Be careful.

Too Much to Do . . . Too Little Time

Extracurricular activities can be another time waster. Much as you try, you can't be PTA president, Little League team mom, homeroom mom, bowling team member, benevolent chairman at the church, Sunday school teacher and sing in the choir too. The ability to say no comes in handy when you see yourself becoming a work horse to every group and organization in town.

Running from early morning until late evening will not make you a very pleasant person to be around. Are you giving the best of yourself to people who in ten years won't even remember your name?

Make guidelines for yourself if this tends to be a problem. Ask yourself:

1. How many nights a week am I out?

2. Am I on the phone when my husband and children are home?

3. What activities do I really enjoy?

4. Why am I doing . . . ?

5. Will what I am doing in these activities matter ten seconds into eternity? Does it help my husband, children, or others in an important way?

6. Does this take away from the priorities in my life?

Preoccupation With the Kids

I can hear the objections on this one: "Pam, I can understand you warning us that many lovers today are working day and night, and many lovers are wasting precious time. But time with the kids? Aren't we supposed to be with them? After all, they need us."

I say, "Yes! *Absolutely* . . . but not *exclusively*."

The danger lies in caring for the kids to the exclusion of maintaining a close romantic relationship with your husband.

We all experience the "new mommy syndrome." The feelings of a sex symbol and a loving, nurturing mommy cannot have residence in the same body. The same parts of a woman's body used to express sexual feelings are also used in giving birth and nurturing the tiny infant.

In the beginning it is difficult to reconcile the changing functions. New daddies don't struggle with these changes. All they see is a body that is no longer pregnant and they assume we are the same as before. We may look like the same woman they married, give or take a few post-natal pounds, but in all fairness we must admit we are not the same.

We have a profound feeling of responsibility, a desire for nurturing this baby. Romantic feelings are difficult to turn on and off. The short walk from the crib, where there is sweetness, innocence and a lullaby, to the bed where there awaits a heavy-breathing man with near animal passion, seems too short a distance to make the transition. There must be time and space allowed to change the feelings and mode of thinking. I suggest being honest with your husband regarding the difficulty in this role change. Plan and allow some time to rethink and deprogram before hopping into bed. Take a shower. Spend a few minutes reading to get your mind in the right frame.

Remember, becoming a mom doesn't mean you stop being a wife. Many women make a mistake right here. They continually put the baby and kids before their man, jumping every time the kids whimper. Your home will be much happier if you let the children know right away that they will not control your house or Mom and Dad.

Some young mothers make the mistake of allowing the baby to sleep in the same room with them for too long a time. It is best not to keep the baby in your bedroom for more than three to four weeks. Do not allow a child to get into the habit of sleeping with you and your husband. It is a difficult habit to break.

Martha, mother of three, admitted keeping all of her

babies in the room with her and her husband until the babies were toddlers. "I was terribly inhibited sexually during these years; a real iceberg," Martha confessed. Her husband grew weary of Martha's cold shoulder. He constantly heard, "Please, hon, don't do that! Johnny isn't sleeping soundly yet," or "You're making so much noise." or "Stop it; not tonight." Her husband chose to have his sexual needs met in the bedroom of another woman . . . a bedroom without children.

It is very important to establish your bedroom as Mom and Dad's special place. It is healthy for a child to see the natural warmth and special relationship which men and women have as husbands and wives. Throughout your children's lives they need to know that Mom and Dad are, before all else, husband and wife. Josh McDowell, author of *The Dad Difference*, has found that children whose parents show affection toward each other are secure children. When the children see loving and affectionate parents who give their marriages top priority, it gives them the confidence that a great marriage is possible.

The two of you can help your child develop into a healthy, balanced adult by staying committed to each other, and taking time to keep your love alive.

I believe in spending time with your children, touching them a lot, loving, praising and encouraging them. They need their special time — time when you show them how very much you love them. But children should always know Mom and Dad's relationship comes first. After all, one day the kids will have someone special of their own to love, and Mom and Dad will be left alone with each other. What you do now in your marriage will determine how happy and fulfilling those empty-nest years will be.

Working Day and Night

Today more than 60 percent of American women work outside of the household.[1] When both partners work at an outside job, someone has to work overtime at home. Children, laundry, cooking, cleaning, shopping, and the dog require a lot of energy. So what do we have left over for intimacy at the end of one of those days? Just that — leftovers! Who has the strength to come up with romantic flourishes and exciting lovemaking when you are bone tired?

What is a woman to do? *Creativity* is the key when both husband and wife work. Take a minute to evaluate your situation and consider these options.

Many women enjoy their careers and want to continue working. If that's you and it's financially feasible, you might hire outside help for the household work. This would limit some of the stress you face as you come home after a long day at work. Just knowing the house is clean, dishes done and laundry put away will give you a freer heart and mind as you spend time with your family. Later in the evening you can relax and enjoy some special time with your special man.

If your family is dependent on your income to meet expenses (making it financially impossible to hire outside help), learn to delegate household duties. Burdens shared are burdens lifted. Children can be taught simple tasks such as making their own beds, sweeping the kitchen floor, helping to dry dishes. As they grow they can assist you by learning to do their own laundry and preparing some family meals. And don't forget Dad. It probably wouldn't kill him to wash dishes once or twice a week! You'll be building a sense of community as you all pitch in to make your house a home.

If it's your heart's desire to stay at home and care

for your family full time, you and your husband should reevaluate your outside work load. Some women feel they are working for nothing after the work-related expenses are tabulated (child care, commuting expenses, work wardrobe, higher taxes, etc.). You and your husband need to calculate what you're bringing home. It may not be as much as you think! Perhaps you could survive on his paycheck alone.

Part-time or flex-time work might be a possibility for you. An in-home job is another option. Here is a list of ideas:

1. Bookkeeping
2. Typing
3. Child care
4. Preparing meals on wheels
5. Baking pies and cookies
6. Sewing
7. Cake decorating
8. Clowns and parties
9. Escort service
10. Telephoning
11. Stuffing envelopes
12. Paying bills for the elderly
13. Board and care home
14. Wedding planner
15. Beautician
16. Arts and crafts

If you are not certain whether working at home is right for you, the book *Moonlighting: 148 Ways to Make Money,* by Carl Houseman, can help you decide.

If you definitely feel you don't want to pursue career and family simultaneously, cutting corners whenever possible helps make this option more feasible. Here are some money-saving tips that came in handy for Richard and me:

1. Do not use credit cards. Live on the budget.

2. Before buying a different car, check on rebuilding the engine and going another 100,000 miles on your present vehicle.

3. Save money for upcoming events like vacations or Christmas. Spend only the cash you have saved. Never purchase consumable or depreciating items on credit.

4. Do not overspend when purchasing a home. Be conservative and realistic. Keep your house payments as low as possible.

5. Certainly give God His part first.

6. To stay organized regarding bills, establish an easy, efficient filing system.

7. Consider paying some bills once a year (like insurance premiums). You can save 10 to 15 percent.

8. Trim the grocery bill by making a list and sticking to it, buying in bulk, using coupons, buying what you need on payday and not making extra trips to the store except for milk and bread. (Money for these can be included in the grocery expense. Put it in a sealed envelope and use only for those items.)

9. Do not eat out so often.

Whether you're working all day caring for your home and family or holding down a job outside of your home, remember to save some quality time for your husband. Many lovers are so tired from working long days that they just fall into bed and forget about love . . . the love that brought all this about in the first place. Let's not work ourselves right out of loving each other.

I remember Marc and Pat, a couple I, as a young bride, placed on a lofty pedestal. This couple really had the good life: a comfy home, two little cherubs named Lisa and Kenny, much love, and enough income to live comfortably without Pat having to work outside the home. She even had time to teach a young bride (me) to make homemade jam and roast a duck, and she gave me some great tips on loving my new husband.

Then Marc was offered a new job in the big city. More money was the reason for pulling up the roots they had planted in the quiet little suburb.

More money almost always means more hours at work, more stress, more demands, more headaches and less time, less energy and less caring for those you love. In this case more money cost Marc everything. The entire family fell apart. He spent his time and energy unwisely; he sold out to a company that promised more money. People usually don't notice the fine print that says, "Oh yes, for more money we expect you to give us everything you've got!"

This is not an isolated story. It happens every day in Your Town, U.S.A. Please, please make time for your partner, the one you love, top priority. Do not sell out for more money.

Personal Challenge

1. Keep this chart for one week, indicating how you spend your leisure time. At the end of a week, add up the time spent in each category and see for yourself what you have been doing. Evaluate these findings with your husband and make adjustments where needed.

- This is for leisure time (after dinner until bedtime). Any days off should be included as well.

- Keep a small note pad with you to write down the activities you are involved in. Example: Help with Mark's homework—7:00-8:30. Talked to Cindy on phone—8:30-8:45.

- Do not alter your week to make the chart look better than it should. Try to live as normally as possible to get the true picture of time you spend in these categories.

- Time with husband means time *alone* with him. Time with other people does not count. Example: Watching a movie can count as time with your husband as long as the kids are not with you. An evening meal is a "family" time, even though your husband is there too.

- In figuring out how you have done, calculate the total hours in your own schedule of leisure time. Example: I have 5:30 to 11:00 p.m., 5 days a week plus one day off (13 hours more) and six leisure hours on Sunday (because Sunday is a work day for those in the ministry) which gives me approximately 46 hours a week. Your leisure time may be quite different from mine.

LEISURE TIME CHART

Activity	Sun.	Mon.	Tues.	Wed.	Thur.	Fri.	Sat.
TV							
Housework							
Family							
Friends							
Husband							
Extra							

(chart time in hour and half-hours only)

2. What were the results of your chart?

Total hours _____ TV

Total hours _____ Housework

Total hours _____ Family

Total hours _____ Friends

Total hours _____ Husband

Total hours _____ Extra activities (crafts, volunteer-ing, reading, choir, etc.)

Be a mistress to your husband
so he'll never find himself
in need of one.

T · H · R · E · E

"Love Me Tender," Please

As a young bride I was quite startled to receive the challenge, "Be a mistress to your husband so he'll never find himself in need of one."

That's advice I intended to use! I had learned how to cook spaghetti, fry crisp finger-lickin'-good chicken, make perfect pie crust and stir up a mean chocolate cake. But the word *mistress* captured my young heart with great interest. I knew I didn't want my marriage on the casualty list. This advice implied I could prevent this from happening. I wanted to major in this subject—being a mistress to my husband!

Just Tell Me How

In my attempt to begin a crash course on the subject, I was disturbed to find very little Christian information. Searching the Christian bookstores for material on "mistressing" didn't take very long. Twenty years ago the selection was meager.

Of course, there was God's Word on the subject —
the Song of Solomon. However, as a young girl I had been
programmed that this was not a real story of sexual love
and romance, but an allegory of Christ and the church.
When I read through its lovingly romantic pages I tried not
to taint its true meaning with sensual thoughts.

At the time, I did not have Joseph Dillow's book,
Solomon On Sex. What an eye-opener that would have
been!

What could I do? Where could I go for information
on this subject? I was desperate to understand how to
become the complete wife I needed to be. I prayed about it:
"Lord, what does a mistress do to satisfy her lover? I don't
want the children of darkness to be wiser on this subject
than this child of light!"

Learn From Every Source You Can

J. Allen Petersen writes, "Pick up every practical
idea you can from every source and creatively apply it to
your relationship. Copy all the good ideas you can and
experiment with them. Practice them!"[1]

Information on the subject of sex in marriage is
certainly more accessible now than it was twenty years ago.
The subject of sexual technique has been boldly approached
by some great Christian authors. No tiptoeing around. It's
very straightforward.

Men and women of the '90s need this information.
We cannot go around with our heads in the sand. Ignorance
isn't winning many battles these days. Consider this in-
sightful saying regarding ignorance versus wisdom:

> He who knows not, and knows not he knows not, he is
> a fool. Shun him.

He who knows not, and knows he knows not, he is simple. Teach him.

He who knows and knows not he knows, he is asleep. Awaken him.

He who knows, and knows he knows, he is wise. Follow him.

With great enthusiasm I applaud the men and women who have written books on the role of sex in a Christian marriage for our benefit. Buy the books that interest you, borrow them from a friend, or beg your church to put them in the church library. Begin to gather information to enrich your marriage *now,* not tomorrow. (There is a list of excellent books for further reading at the end of this chapter.)

I am also aware that there is some extremely offensive junk which tries to pass itself off as the word on sex — pornography. Unfortunately, even some Christians are using it. I, in no way, recommend any of this material. Pornography brings destruction. Avoid it in every form.

A video store owner once told my husband, "My customers getting X-rated videos are young married couples between the ages of twenty-five and thirty-five. These couples seem to have low batteries and need a jump-start to get going!"

Please understand, this is not God's way. You and your husband can be each other's fantasy. There can be complete satisfaction in the area of eroticism with just the two of you. You may need some education and some new ideas, but look for that information in the right places. Plan to be what your husband needs as a sexual partner. Take the time to let him know what you need as well.

The Bible gives some guidelines on how innovative sex can be between husband and wife. Paul tells us in

Corinthians, "Let the husband fulfill his duty to his wife and likewise also the wife to her husband. The wife does not have authority over her own body, but the husband does, and likewise also the husband does not have authority over his own body, but the wife does. Stop depriving one another!" (1 Corinthians 7:3-5).

We must make every effort to be available to each other, willing and wanting to satisfy. After all, isn't marriage the place for those needs to be met?

A very confused young gal in my Bible study group came to me recently. "Pam, I'm a new Christian, and I don't know if it's right to do some of these intimate things with my husband. It doesn't seem very holy," she said.

I told her, "The Lord's very own hand-picked apostle Paul encourages us to relax and enjoy sex. He says in Hebrews 13: 'Marriage is honorable . . . and the bed undefiled.'"

Let go of any guilt feelings. Talk through the things which make you feel uncomfortable. Do not ask things of each other which may lead to an uneasy feeling. This is the "preferring one another in love" spoken of in Romans 12:10.

Preferring — what a great word for love. Considering, caring, compromising my wishes for another. Think about that word, pray for the Lord's guidance, and then decide for yourselves what the guidelines for sex should be. They will vary for different couples and certainly may change through the years as you feel more freedom between the two of you.

Do not compare yourself with other couples. If you are experiencing satisfaction and contentment, do not let anyone else's bragging or big talk make you feel less fulfilled.

God's perfect plan is for the husband and wife to completely meet the sex drive, sexual appetite, and sexual desire in each other. Educate yourself to be his mistress. Keep him coming back for more of you!

See Infidelity as a Real Threat

"Why the big worry, Pam?" you may ask. "I'm married to a wonderful Christian man. He loves God and is the original iron man with his emotions. I trust him completely."

Complete trust is essential in a marriage, but the woman who thinks infidelity could never happen in her marriage is living in a dream world. The Bible warns us over and over that Satan cannot be trusted: "Your enemy the devil prowls around like a roaring lion looking for someone to devour" (1 Peter 4:8). His prey is the naive. You could be his next meal if you close your eyes and hide under the covers!

I am reminded of a young couple I know. Dave and Marty were real go-getters—Bible study leaders, youth workers, choir members and Sunday school teachers. They spent most of their time and energy outside their secular jobs involved in church work.

Strong and handsome Dave never dreamed a nineteen-year-old girl could knock him off his fortified, sacred tower, but she did. This young gal needed some help through a rough time. While Marty was home cutting flannelgraph one night for Sunday school class, Dave was facing a dragon in his life . . . passionate desire. Satan, who knows us so well, had provided the most sensuous bait he could find for Dave.

Nothing wrong with cutting flannelgraph. Nothing wrong with helping a kid through a difficult time. But Marty and Dave were so preoccupied with *doing* that they forgot about *being* with each other, and meeting each other's needs through touching, romance, playful intimacy and sex. I consider these four things the super glue of marriage. Dave now admits, "I wanted it to be Marty kissing and caressing me instead of this young girl. I had no idea how hungry I was for this hot passion, until I got close enough to smell the savory porridge she was cooking up for me. Once I was that close, I could not resist."

J. Allen Petersen warns us: "When needs are not met, the door is opened for infidelity. Someone else will meet those needs."[2]

Family author James Dobson says it adamantly:

> Great needs arise. The greater the needs for pleasure, romanticism, sex, ego satisfaction, the greater the needs within a marriage. . . . [Sometimes] a need accumulates and does not get met. The need gets greater and when the need gets greater, then the voices calling people into infidelity get greater.[3]

We must uncover these needs and know what our lover is desiring from us.

A mistress of the thirteenth and fourteenth century took very seriously her man's likes and dislikes. She studied him and became an expert in what he particularly enjoyed. She specialized in pleasing her lover. The desire to meet his needs was at the top of her priority list.

Let's face it. When it comes to sexual appetites, all men are not created equal. Some men seem to have an unquenchable appetite. Others survive on less. If you are married to Mr. Can't-Get-Enough you need to discover how you can best meet his needs. Being indifferently available is not enough. He needs more than just a consenting corpse. Study your husband well. Be an expert on him. Only then will you truly know how to please him.

The time I've invested in studying the art of mistressing has paid off in an important dividend. My husband of twenty years is helplessly in love and lust with me.

Personal Challenge

1. Read at least one Christian book on the subject of sex. Take notes on things you can use and forget the rest.

2. Look up the word *mistress* in a dictionary. List ways in which your role as wife and lover are similar to her job.

3. If your husband were a paying customer, what specialty of yours in bed would keep him coming back for more?

4. Use the space below to write four or five steps you will take to help you move closer to the goal of being Mrs. Mistress.

(1)

(2)

(3)

(4)

(5)

5. Grade yourself on a scale of 1 to 5 on meeting your husband's needs:

(5) I always say yes and/or initiate sexual play in our relationship.

(4) I will generally say yes and/or initiate sexual play.

(3) I say yes half of the time. I presently do not initiate sexual play.

(2) I say yes usually to avoid an argument.

(1) I admit it, I'm an iceberg! Sex is extremely rare between my husband and me.

How do you think your husband would rate you? You can decide if you get an A +, B, C, D, or F!

6. Write out your commitment to your husband to become his private mistress. (Read this to him when you have completed this book.)

Recommended Reading List

Dillow, Joseph. *Solomon on Sex.* Nashville: Thomas Nelson, 1982.

Hocking, David and Carole. *Romantic Lovers.* Eugene, OR: Harvest House Publishers, n.d.

LaHaye, Tim. *Practical Answers to Common Questions About Sex in Marriage.* Grand Rapids: Zondervan Publishing House, 1984.

LaHaye, Tim and Beverly. *The Act of Marriage.* Grand Rapids: Zondervan Publishing House, 1976.

Mayo, Mary Ann. *A Christian Guide to Sexual Counseling.* Grand Rapids: Zondervan Publishing House, 1989.

Miles, Herbert. *Sexual Happiness in Marriage.* Grand Rapids: Zondervan Publishing House, 1987.

Paulk, Earl. *Sex Is God's Idea.* Denville, NJ: Dimension, 1985.

Penner, Clifford and Joyce. *The Gift of Sex.* Waco, TX: Word Books, 1981.

Wheat, Ed. *Intended for Pleasure.* Old Tappan, NJ: Fleming H. Revell Company, 1981.

F · O · U · R

Wear an "Itsy, Bitsy, Teenie, Weenie" What?

We have already established the fact that you cannot sweep a man off his feet if you are dead on yours. Come alive! Keep your marriage relationship full of vigor and energy.

One area to keep on the front burner is creativity in romance. Do not settle for the ho-hums in your relationship. Decide today to make yourself undeniably unforgettable, extraordinarily exquisite.

Be Alluring

Yes, I know. You have a hard time seeing yourself quite like that. It's time to change those thoughts. Realize that everyday life can be sexier than you think. *Glamour Magazine* recently took a survey and found that men find some pretty ordinary situations extremely sensual:[1]

- "A woman pulling on stockings."
- "Watching her put on a necklace or choose earrings."
- "Seeing her fresh from a shower, in a big robe with hair wet and combed back."
- "Watching her have dinner conversation with other men (proud that she belongs to me and that other men find her interesting)."

I took my own survey and came up with a few more:

- "Watching her walk around in her sexy underwear, especially if we are in a hurry and sex is out of the question. I find myself wanting her all day long."
- "Seeing her quietly sitting alone in front of the fire, her thoughts far away."
- "Painting or cleaning — anything that causes her to bend over."
- "Walking up stairs with me behind her, of course."
- "Our skin in water together, like swimming or sharing a spa or shower."
- "Napping on top of the covers, dressed skimpily."

Perhaps it's time to rethink our everyday life. Make the most of the sexy images that happen around us on a regular basis.

My friend Mary says her husband thinks it is very provocative for her to sleep in his T-shirt. Each night she gets out the clean T-shirt he is planning to wear the next day. She puts his favorite perfume on her freshly showered body, then slips into the T-shirt, and wears sexy panties.

Early the next morning she removes the T-shirt, places it with his clean clothes for the day and puts on her robe until she is ready to get dressed. As Mary's husband goes through the day, the delicate scent of her perfume lingers with him and he feels extremely close to her.

Needless to say, Mary is alluring her husband and quite effectively, I might add. I watch them together and can see this man only has eyes for one very smart lady— Mary with that marvelous T-shirt!

Mystery Scent

Something my friend Mary might not even be aware of is *pheromones*—subtle sexual aromas exuded by mammals. In animals, this aroma acts as a mating device. Although humans do not go around smelling people to find a suitable mate, Stephanie Sanders, of the Kinsey Institution for Research in Sex and Gender and Reproduction, says, "Pheromones exert far more influence over us than we realize. A woman's sense of smell sharpens at mid-cycle—which means her ability to detect her partner's pheromones may be heightened during ovulation, when she's both most aroused and most likely to conceive ... Sexual scents may underlie the undeniable but unexplainable attraction we feel for certain people we've just met."[2]

We bathe, use perfumes, powders, deodorants—and still these pheromones seem to affect us. This must be pretty potent stuff. Perhaps Mary's husband is not smelling the bottled perfume, but the sweet smell that is uniquely Mary's.

The Song of Solomon speaks of a certain fragrance which the two lovers relish and remember even when apart:

Pleasing is the fragrance of your perfumes; your name is like perfume poured out (1:3).

The fragrance of your perfume is better than any spice (4:10*b*).

The fragrance of your garments is like that of Lebanon (4:11*b*).

Many times I have smelled my husband's shirt and felt very stirred up, thinking I would love to have him near me at that moment.

Mary's idea of wearing her husband's T-shirt is one we should all try. I love the idea of my fragrance lingering with my husband Richard all day. Let's make the most of these mysterious pheromones.

Naughty Nighties

I can hardly speak of alluring without mentioning the nighties we choose to sleep in each night. Think back to the week of your honeymoon. You probably did some special shopping. We all wanted everything to be perfect those first nights we spent together.

What about now? Why aren't we just a little bit embarrassed when we take out that wretched rag night after night? You know, the one that is so comfy and broken in. Why is it we will spend money for a new coat because the old one is worn out, but continue to wear ragged panties, bras and nightgowns? Do we care more what others think of our appearance than our own husband? Shouldn't he be the one we wish to please?

Marrilyn's Story. Marrilyn is a friend of mine who shared with me her own sad story of neglect in this area. In the beginning of her marriage, Marrilyn had the right idea. She purchased wonderful see-through nightgowns, bras and panties. Great looking stuff for the eyes of her new groom.

He loved it! As he thought of her throughout his day, he could remember clearly what she had on underneath her clothing. He enjoyed it continually through the instant replay of his mind. He experienced great pleasure in the reruns he had tucked away. He could relive the sensual beauty of his wife at any time, even when she wasn't around.

When Marrilyn was pregnant with their first child, things began to change. She didn't feel all that attractive anymore, and she certainly did not enjoy parading in exotic undergarments in front of her husband. Maternity bras and panties are big, serviceable-looking and comfortable. She wore them throughout her nine months of waiting. After the baby was born, she felt fat and unattractive, not the same alluring person she was before. Besides, she felt very secure—her husband was used to seeing her at her worst, and he stayed around.

About this time Marrilyn began to let down in the sensuality department. After all, she was a mother, and the fun and games had to stop for a few years. She planned on returning to it one day . . . when the children were older.

In the meantime her husband noticed a real void in his life. He missed seeing his wife dressing and undressing in front of him. The pretty bras and panties were only a fading replay in his mind. He loved Marrilyn and wanted to see her in these pretty things once again. The few extra pounds didn't hinder his desire for her. He mentioned this a few times, hoping to convince his wife that he found her as attractive as ever. But by now Marrilyn was quite comfortable with a white terrycloth nightgown. Yes, it did have a few snags and stains, but it served a purpose. She was not ready to go back to the see-through material she once donned.

This was unfortunate, because her husband needed *something* to look at. It started out with girlie magazines, nothing too bad. But as always, Satan had a plan. This husband soon found himself interested in pornographic material. All he really wanted was a good look at his loving wife in something besides comfy, worn-out lingerie.

I am not suggesting we have a gown burning (although some husbands might provide matches if we decided in favor of that). We all have our favorite, warm, snugly jammies, to be sure. But somewhere we need to have a sexy, see-through, sensual outfit we can pull out. We cannot expect our loving and loyal husband to simply bite the bullet. He has a need to be stimulated by sight. Let's take on the assignment to be his one and only alluring sight.

Be Adventuresome

There lives in all of us a desire for adventure, that playful thing we count on to make life fun and entertaining. We should most definitely integrate adventure into our marriage. Without real thought and planning, it may not come. Adventure rarely happens on a regular basis without someone taking time and effort to help it along.

Tim Stafford recently wrote, "Many Christian marriage partners are in love, but not happy."[3]

How can this be? These couples have simply lost their ability to have fun in their marriage.

Couples should look for opportunities in their lives to have some plain ol' fun. Family therapist Michael Metz, of the University of Minnesota Medical School, says, "Playfulness captures the essential features of intimacy. It is vital for healthy interaction."[4]

One study found that the more time couples spent together in activity, such as eating, playing and just talking, the more satisfying the marriage. This same article also mentions that sex is the most powerful source of private play because it allows for experimentation, relaxation and closeness.[5]

We must initiate new ways to let go and have fun

with each other. That is where adventure comes in. Whether it is a frivolous frolic in the park or a well-planned weekend away from home, it is essential to the well-being of our marriages.

I have some true stories to share with you, given to me by women who believe adventure is an important part of their marriage.

Jane's Story

I wanted to do something extra special for my husband on Valentine's Day. Something wild and crazy that he would not soon forget. After much thought and some input from a friend, I struck upon the perfect idea—a balloon dance!

Early on the fourteenth I spent the morning blowing up small balloons of various shapes and sizes. Afterwards, I tied them to several lengths of string and fashioned them into an outfit.

When my husband Tom came home from work we enjoyed a nice meal with our two children and celebrated Valentine's Day as a family. We put the kids to bed early so we could spend the rest of the evening together . . . alone.

I told Tom to go to the bedroom and he would find a surprise from me under his pillow. Under the pillow I left a set of instructions fastened with a diaper pin. The instructions told him to get ready for bed, hold the diaper pin in his hand, and wait for me to appear.

After a reasonable amount of time, I entered the bedroom humming the song, *The Stripper*. I did a tantalizing dance wearing only my balloon outfit. By that time, the purpose of the diaper pin became quite obvious.

A cute twist to this story is that the diaper pin

came in very handy when, in just nine months to the day, we had a delightful baby boy. That was a Valentine's Day my husband would not soon forget!

Pam's Story

My husband Richard's thirtieth birthday was coming up and I just had to make it unforgettable. He is a busy pastor, and his schedule is jam packed. He has to plan for weeks in advance for any kind of getaway. So I decided to kidnap him.

I made reservations at a wonderful bed and breakfast place that resembled Tara from *Gone With the Wind.* It was especially fun to go behind his back to rearrange his schedule. Each night I had to check his Day-Timer to make certain his secretary could cancel any appointment on the kidnapping date.

The tenth of October drew near and the entire church staff was in on the kidnapping. We passed notes secretly, made anonymous phone calls and generally had a great time keeping Richard in the dark.

Finally, the big day arrived. I prepared breakfast for the family in my usual way, got the kids off to school, and kissed my birthday boy good-bye, wishing him a great day at the office. As soon as he was out of sight, I began to fly through the house, getting his private toiletries packed and ready for our big rendez-vous.

I placed the suitcases in the trunk of the car so he would not see them. I dressed up in my very best outfit, and off I went to steal the pastor of the Baptist church.

I arrived around ten o'clock that morning. I knocked on his door, walked in and said I needed him to go somewhere very important with me. He obliged, and out the door we went.

No one in the office let on anything was up. I took the driver's seat; he rode shotgun. I headed straight for the freeway, which unnerved him to some degree. He said, "Hon, what are you doing? Where are we going? You know I have a lot of meetings and appointments today that I need to get back to."

I smiled and kept heading straight down the freeway. By this time he was actually sweating.

After we had been driving for about an hour (an hour filled with sweet reflections of his thirty years), he figured I was up to no good and had resolved to wait and see where this crazy, impetuous wife of his was taking him.

As we pulled up to the mansion, he actually turned white.

"What is this, Pam? I can't believe my eyes. It looks like something from a fairy tale," he exclaimed.

When the bellhop escorted us to our fabulous bedroom, a throwback to the pre-Civil War days, Richard was elated.

We had the most memorable twenty-four hours of our married life. The atmosphere, the adventure and the accommodations were intoxicating. We delighted in each other every possible moment.

He brings up this wonderful day from time to time, and always thanks me for the effort it took to pull off this unforgettable adventure.

Tammy's Story

It was Valentine's Day. My husband Rob and four other men got together to plan a surprise dinner for the wives. All we were told was to block out that day for something special, and to go buy a new outfit. We weren't even told that other couples were involved.

On the night of the date, my husband began cooking up a wonderful-looking green bean dish. In order not to spoil the surprise that he apparently had for me, I decided not to ask any questions.

After I got dressed for the occasion, Rob drove me out to a home in the country. I had never been there before, and was wondering where we were headed. When I entered the house, there were four other wives, all wearing new dresses and looking just as baffled as I.

The lovely home where this meal took place belonged to the parents of one of the wives. Her mother was in on the surprise. She helped the men along by spreading her beautiful dining room table with her best china, linens and a freshly cut bouquet of flowers.

The men served us in style. They had chilled sparkling cider to toast us as "the best of the best lovers in the world."

Each husband had prepared a portion of the dinner himself. (This proved to us that our men were much more capable in the kitchen than they had let on.) We saw how much they truly loved us because we understood the time it took to prepare for this gorgeous gourmet meal. We will always remember the extravagant arrangements.

The evening meal began with a relish tray like I had never seen before, complete with bay shrimp in chili sauce. We dined on sword fish, wild rice, fancy green beans, a delightful tossed salad, rolls and cherries jubilee (flame and all). The evening was topped off by steaming cups of rich coffee and a wonderfully romantic movie.

We wives were so impressed by this display of affection that we called up the local newspaper and had the entire affair written up in the Metro section. We truly wanted to express our appreciation for what our husbands had done for us, all on their own.

These stories can inspire and motivate us to be creative in our marriages. In Song of Solomon 7:11, we read of a spontaneous wife who whisks her lover away to the countryside. They spend the night and enjoy the wonderful view and refreshing aroma of the vineyards.

I hope these adventures have inspired you to come up with a few endeavors of your own for your special man.

A few other ideas:

Leave a steamy note in the shower for him, explaining in detail what you plan on doing to him when he gets home that evening.

When your husband has to go away on a business trip, pack a pair of sexy undies in his suitcase. Hide them among his clothes so he will discover them as he unpacks. (This is especially fun if he is rooming with one of his colleagues.) The undies will keep you on his mind the entire time he is away.

Sometimes we desperately need a change of scenery, but cash is low and the budget doesn't show signs of improvement. If that's your situation, you might try something my friend and I did a few years ago. I changed my bedroom into a lovely haven, complete with pretty sheets, freshly cut flowers, chilled sparkling cherry cider, and a candle to help create the mood. Richard and I arrived at our friends' home with our overnight bag, ready to stay with their boys while they spent an intoxicating evening in our bedroom, a few blocks away. In a few weeks they returned the favor. She even made a scrumptious salad and rolls for us. It was exciting to be somewhere besides our own bedroom. The best part was the price: time and effort given in love by a friend.

Adventure may take some effort, but the dividends are well worth the time you invest.

Be Allowing

Do you remember the old song "I'm in the Mood for Love?" Well, are you? What gets us in the mood anyway?

Scientists are discovering that there is such a thing as "sexual chemistry." This "chemistry" can, on a daily basis, affect when we feel sexually aroused. It has to do with our hormones. Most women think it is estrogen which governs our desire. But not so, say the experts.

Research psychologist Barbara Sherwin, of McGill University in Montreal, found that the hormone testosterone, known as the male hormone, is responsible for these feelings.[6] You may not have realized it, but women have testosterone in their bodies as well. This hormone is the energizer of our sexual desire. Take it away and the sex drive dies.

Dr. Sherwin will often prescribe testosterone along with estrogen to women who have had a complete hysterectomy. These patients experience a noticeable increase in sexual desire, and report feeling stronger, more energetic and in higher spirits. It appears we do not need an extensive amount of this hormone to make our body function at its best. But we certainly do need it to keep us on an even keel.

Ever wonder why your husband is in the mood in the morning, and you aren't? Because testosterone is at its peak in the morning.

We women tend to allow what's going on around us to alter the peak we experience in the morning. We are programmed to get up, get breakfast, get dressed, get the kids dressed, etc. By the time we have done all these things, our peak is already passed.

But all is not in vain. We have a monthly peak as well—twelve to fourteen days after our monthly period begins, which is when we ovulate. Isn't it marvelous how God put us together? He gave us an inborn heightened sexual desire right when we are most likely to conceive. So if you are planning a honeymoon getaway, I would suggest going mid-cycle. Timing can be the deciding factor between a so-so time and a great time away.

Toward the end of your menstrual cycle a neurotransmitter called serotonin kicks in and acts like a sexual suppressant. So there really are times you just don't feel like having sex.

I can hear the yeas and hoorahs right about now: "I finally have an excuse to say no and not feel bad about it." Not exactly. Our sexual relationship is a gift we give to each other. As 1 Corinthians 7 tells us, our body belongs to our husband and his body belongs to us. Sex between husband and wife is to be given as a gift—not demanded, withheld or used as a reward or punishment.

My husband has a minister friend who walks on egg shells constantly. His wife tells him he had better comply to all her wishes or there will be no sex. He is one frustrated individual.

Using sex as a means of getting things your way is a very selfish act. Sometimes you may not be super turned-on to the idea of a romp in the hay, but this is the time to put aside your feelings. Put your effort into satisfying his needs. Allow your husband to enjoy you and your marvelous love — love that you alone are allowed by our Father to give your husband. You may be surprised how this can put you in the mood.

Being married doesn't mean the fun has to stop. Take a chance. Buy a skimpy little nightie and surprise your husband tonight. Plan a getaway for the two of you and then do it. Rekindle the romance of your love. You'll be on your way to a happier, long-lasting relationship.

Personal Challenge

1. Try to incorporate at least one of the everyday sensual images listed at the beginning of this chapter into your daily routine.

2. Look closely at your lingerie. If you do not have something *very* sexy and alluring, go shopping!

3. If you do have something sexy in your lingerie drawer, great. Why not get a little crazy? Buy that outrageous-looking red teddy or black bikini underpanties. Spice up your same ol' tune.

4. Plan in detail an exciting adventure for you and your husband, then carry it out. Don't ever, ever stop planning adventure for your relationship.

5. Monitor your mood swings and determine when you think your testosterone is at its peak. Use this information in planning dates with your husband. If you have had a hysterectomy and feel out of sorts most of the time, check with your gynecologist regarding possible hormone treatment.

Your bedroom decor
is a testimony of your love
for each other.

$F \cdot I \cdot V \cdot E$

"This Ol' House" Needs Some Romance!

A few years ago my family was visiting in the home of some friends of ours for a day of swimming and sunning and barbecuing. When we had all the water our bodies could stand for one day, we migrated to the bedrooms and bathrooms to change into dry clothing.

Every room had been carefully groomed for our visit that day. Every room except the one I was told to use . . . the master bedroom—that special room where husband and wife would meet each night for rest, refreshment and romance.

As I opened the door, my eyes fixed upon a horrendous sight. This room bore no resemblance to a bedroom at all, except for a bed against the side wall. As I sought for a place to disrobe, I could not help but see what this room had become. It was one of the most unkempt storage rooms I've ever seen.

To the left was a dresser, Early American design I think. It was covered with old newspapers. (If you should need a magazine dating back ten years or more, I know where you can find it.) The dresser sagged from the weight of the paper piled two feet on top. The drawers were half opened with clothes sticking out here and there.

As my eyes scanned the rest of the room, I noticed a mountainous pile of clothes lying next to an ironing board. It looked like ironing for a family of twenty. (There were only four residing here.)

Moving right along, my eyes rested on an old rattan bird cage which the resident had vacated, but the evidence that he had been there was still very obvious.

There were mounds of clothing about the room looking like the owner had quickly stepped out of one item to put on another. The room was dark, dingy, depressing and actually very dirty.

But the most curious sight of all was the bed itself. Smack in the middle of this queen-size bed, nestled *between* the sheets, lay a massive German shepherd. This was most certainly his territory – the room reeked with dog odor.

I must have set a record that day in speed dressing. I could not get out of that room fast enough. I now viewed my host and hostess in a new light.

I noticed they were not courteous to each other. They never touched or exchanged glances of gratitude. In fact, they did not seem even remotely fond of each other. This all added up after having visited their love nest.

The room I just described is probably the only one of its kind anywhere. But just in case your love nest is being neglected, let's talk about the bedroom.

Bumpy Bed?

K Mart tells us, "If you can make a bed, you can decorate a room."

Your bed represents a place of intimacy. It's not the *only* place to make love, but it is the most obvious. Therefore, attraction must be considered a priority when choosing how you put it together.

The sheets should be clean, even if they can't be new. A light powdering can make them fresh and inviting. Scented sheets are not new in creating an enticing bedroom; women of the 14th century used to sprinkle rose petals on their beds to make them smell wonderfully romantic. Solomon even perfumed his carriages with myrrh and spices. His beloved speaks of wonderful fragrance being spread everywhere, letting many delicious scents flow to allure her lover (Song of Solomon 4:16).

If your budget will allow, invest in satin sheets (even the synthetic ones feel quite sensual). Make this place your private quarters, the most sumptuous piece of furniture in the house.

When people visit our home they generally comment on how beautiful our bed is. The bed itself is cream-colored porcelain with ornate flowers and hearts woven together. I have sheets, bed ruffle, comforter and pillow shams to match. Throw pillows of all shapes and sizes enhance the beauty of the ensemble.

This bed was a dream we had for many years before we could purchase it. In the early days of extra-tight budgets, I had to improvise to create a pretty picture. Our first bed didn't have a headboard at all. I just had lots of pretty handmade pillows and all of the teddy bears that Richard bought for me while we were dating. (In five years you accumulate a lot of stuffed animals!) That was our great-looking headboard.

I kept the sheets clean and aromatic. Sometimes I would turn the covers back and place an expensive chocolate on my love's pillow to give him extra energy.

If you have the money to invest in a gorgeous masterpiece bed, buy it. The investment pays off well.

When choosing the type of bed you would like to have, shop around. Look for bedroom arrangements in furniture stores, catalogs and magazines, and pay attention in the homes of people you visit. For many years I had a dream file filled with pictures of beds I had seen in magazines.

Which style best suits you and your husband? Which is most attractive? Colonial? Elegant French? Italian? Traditional, modern, contemporary? Perhaps you love the wonderful antique beds which create a romantic mood all their own. Is it a style you can live with for many years? This will be a major investment, so make sure it is what you want.

If you have a so-so bed, don't give up on making it look romantic. Add to its beauty whenever you can.

Walls Wretched?

Bedrooms were called "performance rooms" in the mistress's house a few hundred years ago. I find this term most interesting. Sleeping was done there as well, but the major emphasis in the privacy of that room was on the physical relationship. Detailed murals portraying the love that could be anticipated in the room were found painted above doorways and on the walls.

What do you see displayed on the walls of your bedroom? Something romance-oriented? Or are they filled with family pictures of your kids beginning at age one? I personally prefer not to have the children staring at me when I'm being intimate with my husband. If the pictures are there, it is sometimes difficult to free your mind of the motherly feelings that could inhibit you. Reserve the walls of your bedroom for pictures which create the mood for romance.

My room is decorated in the French country style. There is a picture of a lovely maiden sitting on the steps of a splendid old French home. The maiden is delicate, and the colors are softly muted to create a romantic mood. Near the picture is a dried flower arrangement tied with a ribbon.

I am one who believes in the beauty of memories. Nostalgia is of utmost importance to me, keeping my heart and mind fresh with the days of "wine and roses." I reserve one wall just for a collage arrangement filled with treasures from the past.

I purchased a large frame and put together the story of our courtship. In this frame is a headline from an old teen magazine that says, "The Supremes" (a real hot group of the sixties). Richard's school decal, De Anza Dons, is there also, along with a love letter from me at age fifteen to Richard, age seventeen. My driver's permit and tassel from the graduation hat I wore in 1969 completes this picture.

Every time I look at this collage I am reminded of a beautiful time in our lives. It says over and over again that we were young and in love. I want that love to remain strong and grow more intense every day for the rest of our lives.

The most alluring picture of all should be that which resides just above your bed. It most definitely should be something you consider romantic.

Our quiet, romantic picture is an enchanting lake

scene with a picturesque portrait of a young man rowing a boat, his sweetheart aboard. He is looking at her with all the love one can imagine.

Along with the artful pictures on your walls, you should also create the idea of intimacy from the colors you put together. You can accomplish this by using a wall covering of some kind. Wallpaper is the most common, but stencilling and decorative sheets hung from ceiling to floor can also make the room appealing.

Take time to look through many decorating books. These have colors put together to give you ideas. Place all the ones which look interesting to you in a file. When you are ready to begin decorating, you will have many pre-approved ideas at your fingertips.

Color is a key factor in creating the feeling of warmth and love. *Monochromatic* is different shades and tints of one color. *Analogous* is using corresponding colors next to each other on the color wheel. *Complementary* uses colors opposite each other on the color wheel. *Advanced* has no limits or rules on the number of colors used. Choose whatever suits *your* fancy. Just color it into a haven of love.

Mirrors are a fun way to enhance your private space. They create the illusion of length or depth, actually making the room look more spacious. They also reflect light and silhouettes most interestingly.

Decor Drab?

How you choose to decorate your bedroom will set the atmosphere. It is presently what you desire it to be? Have you spent more money on rooms in the house that catch visitors' eyes and skimped on decorating your own bedroom?

From the bed, which we have discussed in detail, to

the tables you choose, always let the results speak of love. Bed tables can be adorned with romantic lamps and fresh cut flowers from time to time. They might also hold pictures of you and your husband together, or trinkets collected through the years which have a unique story.

I have a special gift from my husband, given to me in Hawaii a few years back. That was a trip I'll always treasure. It was actually something we had promised ourselves for our tenth wedding anniversary. We saved and worked and saved some more until we finally had the money in the bank.

About this time in our lives the Lord directed us to move to a city three thousand miles away and begin a mission church. The finances had to be raised on itinerary. Richard traveled for weeks to present this need to many churches and was able to secure *almost* all of the money needed to begin the new church.

All, except for a small amount. The same amount we had in the bank for our Hawaiian honeymoon.

Neither of us had the courage to mention the money at first, but in prayer one morning the subject came up and we placed the savings passbook on the altar.

We started the work God called us to do and forgot about the honeymoon for our tenth anniversary.

Five years later a friend called Richard and told him he had purchased several package trips to Hawaii as work incentives for his employees. However, one trip wasn't earned, yet it was paid for. You guessed it! The Lord gave us our trip to Hawaii.

So, the little gift that sits on our bed table is of great value to both Richard and me. Each time I steal a glance at this special ornament, I remember what an exotic time we had together on the Islands.

In decorating, remember:

- Have a long-range plan.
- Choose your colors and furniture wisely.
- Utilize wallpaper, paint or stencilling.
- Don't forget fresh cut flowers.
- Lighting is important to create mood.
- Choose romantic pictures.
- Try some nostalgia.
- Create interesting groupings on bedside tables.
- Use candles, mirrors, potpourri, treasure trinkets.
- Do not allow your bedroom to become a storage room!
- Your bedroom should be filled with treasured memorabilia reminding you that two people, very much in love, reside here.

Atmosphere Atrocious?

According to Webster, atmosphere is "the mass of air, clouds, gases surrounding the earth and any other place." Through the decades we have come to use the word in a different way. It is the feeling one experiences through sight, sound and smell in the space he is inhabiting. Much can be said for those who create the right atmosphere before plunging into any important event.

When my daughter Apryl wants to borrow the car, she spends time tactfully meeting my every need. She wants me cool, comfortable and cooperative. Her plan is to be most winsome, and it usually works.

My other daughter Amy is a cheerleader. She works very hard during football and basketball games to create an atmosphere of excitement and euphoric electricity.

We have a quiet time of worship at the conclusion of Sunday services. A soft, compelling hymn is sung reverently to create the atmosphere so quiet, grateful hearts can thank their Father for His many blessings.

We create some type of atmosphere in and around our home and family every day. We choose what it will be. Is it perfect for the mood we want to encourage, or just a blasé nothingness which doesn't touch or move us in the least?

Creating the mood for ecstasy can come through viewing the beauty of art seen in the pictures on the wall. It can be felt through music, as the pulsating beat moves our very soul. Atmosphere can be enhanced by the fragrance of perfumes, scented candles or fresh flowers filling the room with an intoxicating desire.

Do your private quarters reveal the sweet, passionate love that two people residing there feel for one another? Or does your room have the atmosphere of an attic storage area or a workroom where all the undone laundry and ironing gets dumped? Take my advice and dump it someplace else. Make your bedroom a true fantasy world for you and your husband!

Personal Challenge

1. What do you need to do to improve your bed? If you do not have a dream bed pictured, begin your search for one today.

2. Look at the walls of your bedroom. Decide what has to go and what you can use to create a romantic atmosphere. Have at least *one* bit of nostalgia somewhere. Dig it out and start to enjoy the beauty of memories.

3. How are the colors in this room? Do you need to paint, wallpaper or get creative? Remember your file on the perfect bed? Add pictures of the perfect room to it.

4. Do you need to invest in new sheets, blankets or comforter? Do not allow these to get threadbare before replacing them.

5. Do you have candles, romantic lighting and music available in this room? Work specifically on the atmosphere you wish to create. Ask yourself, "How does this room make me feel when I walk through the door? Does it say what I want it to about our love for one another? Is it clearly evident that I consider it the most important room in the house?" If not, go to work on it today.

S · I · X

So "You've Lost That Lovin' Feeling"?

*T*here is so much more to communication than just words! Many non-verbal cues also convey acceptance or rejection, love or lethargy, to our mate.

Look Before You Leap!

One of the most important aspects of communication is eye contact. In the movie *The Karate Kid,* the master teacher would not teach the young student any new karate moves until he first had eye contact with him. The teacher would say, "Look eyes. Always look eyes."

We have adopted this saying in our family. When we want to express something of importance and the listener is not giving us full attention, we say, "Look eyes. Look eyes." It usually brings a smile of acknowledgment and undivided attention.

Eyes can reveal if someone is sad, hurting, angry, cheerful, curious, guilty or overflowing with joy. Eyes can often tell you what's inside a person.

I remember sitting in church as a child, chatting most inconspicuously with my friend Sandy. She was my best friend and there was always so much I needed to tell her. We went to different schools so church was our common ground in catching up on the latest news.

I could pull this off pretty well through the singing time of the service, but when my father went to the pulpit to begin his sermon, I always seemed to get caught. My mother managed to catch my attention and give me the eye. She did not say one word verbally, but in one look I heard her loud and clear: "PAMALA! You had better hush up that whispering and stop writing notes *right now,* or I'll come right over and march you back here to sit with me. And when you get home, you'll get it good!"

This one look was enough to keep me quiet through the entire sermon.

Eyes do speak. We use them to communicate mood, emotion, words unspoken. When we verbalize, we need to make a conscientious effort to use our eyes in a positive way. There are people who cannot look me in the eyes when I am speaking to them. Perhaps as children they did not practice the "look eyes" philosophy, and now as adults they find it difficult to look into someone's eyes. Eyes reveal much and therefore some people refuse to allow eye contact.

It usually takes a while to feel comfortable letting your eyes speak, but it is an excellent way to begin a deeper level of communication with your spouse. Talk about "looking eyes" with him and see what new areas open up to you through this avenue of communication.

Tender Touch Means Sooo Much!

Another form of communication is touching. To reach out and touch someone is best done with a part of your body, not the telephone! Generally, your hand is the best choice.

A soft gentle touch or pat says, "It's all right. I understand. I'm here." A tender stroke can bring calmness to soothe pain or distress. It relaxes. A grabbing motion might mean, "I'm in trouble," or "Look out! Danger ahead!"

There is a distinct sensual touch as well. It speaks clearly of desire, passion, love. You can rub or stroke your lover's hand, leg, face (or whatever) in a language understood by the other person.

Touching another human being is very intimate. You can communicate a message without speaking one word.

Everyone has an inborn need to be touched. If you are not a touching person, work at it. This gesture will make your husband feel closer to you. Touch his shoulder or arm lovingly when saying something directly to him.

Karen's husband Bob grew up in a home where it was taboo to touch anyone. The entire household just spoke when any communication was needed. Bob could *never* remember being touched by his mother, father, or either one of his sisters.

Karen's family was quite different. They hugged and kissed and caressed on a daily basis. When Bob first married into this family he wasn't too sure about all of this touching business. In fact, the first time Karen's brother Mark gave Bob a big hug, he almost got punched out! The experience was that foreign to Bob.

To Bob's delight, everyone kept touching and hugging him until he felt comfortable. Now he is one of the most affectionate members of Karen's family.

He told her, "I want our kids to be raised with all of this touching. It makes a person feel sooo loved! Don't ever stop touching me in that special way, please."

It might take a while before this new and different way of communication feels natural, but it is well worth the effort. Just ask Bob!

Body Lingo

How you present your body while speaking is also a means of communicating a message. Is your posture rigid, revealing a relentless attitude? Do you slouch, showing an unsure disposition? Can you stand or sit with shoulders broad, head up and face forward in a manner most convincing? Or is it a nose in the air, shrug of shoulders, "I am not approachable" attitude? Does your body reveal a disposition of defeat, deficiency, dread, disgruntlement? Or are you demonstrating determination, dignity and delight? The way you carry yourself communicates a message before you speak one word verbally.

Perhaps at times you state in body lingo that you are on the warpath, putting your spouse on the defensive even before he knows what the conversation is about. Practice entering the room with non-offensive body lingo. He will then more openly listen to your carefully chosen words.

The other day I had an exceptionally busy schedule. I gave my two teenage daughters duties to accomplish in my absence. We had to be somewhere soon after I returned home that afternoon, so it was important for them to follow through with the assigned tasks.

When I returned home I immediately noticed one of

Amy's chores was not completed. She was to take the garbage can from the front yard and put it in the side yard where it belonged. I thought, *Aha! They haven't done their work.*

I literally barged into the house with every muscle in my body screaming, even though I hadn't said a word. Both Amy and Apryl began to yell and point fingers and cry and stomp in defense of the uncompleted task.

I caused all of this commotion without saying one word. If I had entered calmly, relaxed and ready to listen to the reason why the job wasn't completed (I found out later there was a legitimate reason), none of this calamity would have taken place.

Many times we speak so loudly with body lingo that our words cannot be heard. The body language has already created a defensive atmosphere, and no one stands a chance of properly understanding our words. This is why so many talks end up going nowhere. The atmosphere is not conducive to receive the message, so end of conversation.

Frustration sets in. The assumption is, "He just won't talk to me." Of course he won't. He can't hear what you are saying because your body language is screaming so loudly.

Listen very closely to the lingo your body is sending out. Is it speaking the words you intend to say verbally? Check up on your body lingo.

Voice Vibes

The way in which we speak words can change the message entirely. For example, take the phrase, "I can't believe you did this." I can say this in a surprised way to express delight. Or I can say it with a disappointed tone in my voice and change the message entirely. I can also say this same phrase with force and indignation to create a completely different message.

I grew up hearing the old cliché, "It's not *what* you say, but *how* you say it." Words do make a difference, but the manner in which you allow those words to come out of your mouth may determine whether the person will listen or tune out. How do you sound? If you ask someone how you generally come across, the answer might be quite shocking.

I have heard women speak with the tone of an army sergeant, commanding the squad to do her bidding and do it *now!* I also have listened to women pitifully squeak an intimidated whisper, only to be totally ignored. I don't recommend either of these approaches. Be aware of *how* your words are coming across.

Hearing Impaired

Just as important as your body language and voice vibes is how the listener actually hears what you are saying. The interpretation of the message you are giving is as important as how you say it. What is coming across to the listener? Is he following your train of thought? Can he understand the words you have chosen to communicate this message?

Garage sales are a common sight in our town. Early one Saturday morning my four-year-old son Aaron and I passed several in progress and I noticed Aaron observing intently while in deep thought.

Soon the *biggest* garage sale I've ever seen came into view. Aaron could not hold back his excitement a minute longer. He smiled in deep satisfaction and sighed as he exclaimed, "Those are so much fun, Mom. Look at all that stuff! When are we gonna have a *garbage* sale?"

Aaron truly thought they were called garbage sales. That's what he arrived at through what he saw and a word he thought he heard correctly.

My daughter Amy called her shoes "shoe-ons" for years. Every time she heard the word *shoes*, it was used in the phrase, "Get your shoes on, Amy," or "Are your shoes on, Amy?" To her they were shoe-ons. That's what her ears heard.

How our listener interprets our message is just as important as the words and ways we use to communicate.

Sometimes *his* thoughts have already decided what we are going to say. This is why we must think through to *whom* we are speaking, and his *frame of mind* when we begin an important conversation.

After an exhausting day at work, your husband needs some time to recover. Do not expect him to be at his listening best the minute he walks through the door. He may or may not remember what you say.

Consider what is going on in your husband's life before you bring up a serious subject. If he has a lot on his mind he will, more than likely, only pick up part of what you say. When he forgets something extremely relevant regarding that conversation, you will be disappointed, despondent and upset.

Plan an appropriate time for those serious talks. A relaxed and refreshed listener will respond to your message much better.

Bend Before You Break!

I grew up in Oklahoma where high winds and tornadoes are a threat every spring. In my grandma's back yard we had a big mulberry tree that had a marvelous tree swing hanging from it. The limbs were strong and the trunk huge. My cousins and I would play under the shade of this tree for hours on end.

I remember vividly the way that tree would bend in the wind. As we waited for the threat of a tornado to pass by, the winds would rage through the little farm. I could see the tree from the kitchen window, wondering if it would survive the storm. As the wind blew furiously, the old tree would bend over and almost touch the ground. The branches looked as if they were bowing down to a mighty king. They would swing and sway as the wind ripped, roared and ravished almost everything in its path.

When the storm was over, Grandpa would go and check the damage done. He would find many trees that had snapped in two from the fierce wind. But the mighty mulberry stood unbroken. It looked even stronger than before.

Perhaps it was the respect we had for that tree which made it appear stronger. We had seen it survive those wretched wind storms. It would bend to keep from breaking.

My grandparents have gone to be with Jesus now. The farm has been sold. But to this day the mighty mulberry still stands in the yard of a little farm in Salina, Oklahoma.

Many other trees on that farm became firewood because they stood rigid, refusing to bend when the mighty storm came. They could not match the strength of the wind and were broken.

There will be definite times in our marriages when the strong winds of disagreement will hit. What we choose to do during these times determines whether we will break or will be standing when the storm blows over.

If the mighty mulberry had stood firm, defiantly refusing to give into the wind, it would be firewood today.

Refusing to compromise during disputes will cause you to lose in the end. What good are you to anyone if you are broken in pieces? Do you want to end up a pile of firewood? Or would you like to stand majestically after the storm, smiling and singing, because you had the strength to bend when it was necessary?

To bend is to admit, "Someone has to give in. I will."

Bending is saying, "I'm sorry," "I'm wrong," "I understand your point of view. Let's do it your way."

Bending may mean swallowing your pride on occasion. It may mean you have to go the extra mile to seek out your spouse and end the silent war.

Bending may cause you to count to ten before answering a loaded retort.

Bending may mean you must learn to live on a disciplined budget because you are married to Tom Tightwad.

Bending is one of the most unselfish and the most difficult acts you will ever be called upon to do. But in the end you will have a better marriage because you were strong enough to bend.

Understand Yourself

Several things must be understood in the area of communication. One important aspect has to do with our own body chemistry. There are times during the month in which a woman's body goes through certain changes that actually camouflage who we are. Our personality takes on a new face. This fact about the female gender causes our male counterparts to shake their heads in utter dismay and confess, "Women. I'll never understand them!"

Rightfully so, since we have difficulty knowing our own selves a few days each month. Some of us notice

changes a couple of days prior to menstruation —
premenstrual syndrome.

Some women are irritable, edgy and crabby. Others
become extremely insecure, wanting and needing inten-
sified closeness. Emotions are on the edge and tears come
without warning. During this time I can cry through every
movie I see, as well as those touching McDonald's commer-
cials! How many women have regretted that impulsive
"yes" to a new and crazy hair style because of that strange
mood which thrust them into needing a change of some
sort — *today!*

Why do we act the way we do? Hormones. They rise,
they fall, they explode, they increase, they decrease. They
are needed and necessary, but above all they are infuriating, aren't they? We are not alone in the effects of these
changes in our body. Generally the entire household suf-
fers, especially our husband. I suggest the following to help
this time run more smoothly:

1. Vitamin B6 — 100 mg. three times per day starting
   seven to ten days prior to the onset of your period.
   (Vitamin B plays an important role in brain me-
   tabolism.) Best dietary sources are brown rice,
   whole grains, nuts, beef, bananas. Avoid salt,
   monosodium glutamate, processed foods, chips,
   soy sauce, canned meats.

2. Vitamin E for symptoms of breast tenderness and
   swelling — 800 to 2000 I.U. (international units)
   per day. Avoid caffeine in products such as coffee,
   tea, chocolate and colas.

3. Reduce stress as much as possible seven to ten
   days prior to your period. Exercise will aid in
   stress reduction.

4. Help fight fatigue by reducing your sugar intake. Eat six small meals during the day. Avoid overeating and stay off sugar.

5. Decrease body fat and improve your weight. This seems to help normalize certain hormones. It also improves your frame of mind.

6. Medications such as Motrin can help eliminate pain brought on from cramping.

7. Prayer. All of life needs the help that prayer can bring, even PMS.

8. Talk to a physician to get the correct diagnosis for you. Some women need hormone supplements. Seek out help if you are feeling any extreme depression or anxiety. You may be suffering due to an imbalance of hormones. Get more than one opinion. I know of women who have lost their families because of an improper hormone level. They lost complete control, making life a nightmare for everyone. Don't just bite the bullet and hope that you get better on your own. If you follow the suggestions above and get no relief, see a doctor soon.[1]

Understanding your body aids in your ability to communicate with your husband. Check the calendar. Is it your time of irrationality? Do things appear bigger or worse today than they really are? Where are you in your hormone cycle? All of this plays an important part in how you approach things. Perhaps things are colored over for a few days but will seem quite all right next week. Take time out to understand these changes. Relax and let go of the pressing situation until life gets on an even keel again.

It is so important that you and your husband work

at communicating. You can have a so-so marriage, one that merely exists, or you can have a marriage that is truly heaven on earth if you both work at real communication. Don't lose that lovin' feeling. Keep it going strong for a lifetime.

Personal Challenge

1. Are you practicing the look eyes formula in communication? Today, make it a point to look into your husband's eyes when you talk with him.

2. How would you rate your touching power? Do you touch your husband when you speak to him:
    A. Constantly?
    B. Usually?
    C. Pretty often?
    E. Rarely?
    F. Never?

3. What is your body lingo saying? Rate yourself 1 to 10 on each question below, 10 being very strong and 1 being weak in that area.
    A. Are you approachable?
    B. Are you convincing?
    C. Are you cold and indifferent?
    D. Are you loving and warm?
    E. Are you defensive?
    F. Are you calm and relaxed?

4. What best describes your tone of voice?
    A. Sergeant Screamer?
    B. Bellowing Bitty?

C. Squawking Shrew?

D. Chiding Chirps?

E. Whispering Willow?

F. Candy Calm?

G. Gentle Gem?

5. What do you think about your bending ability? Write out an incident in which you were the one bending to keep from breaking up a relationship.

S · E · V · E · N

Who Says, "You Ain't Nothin' But a Hound Dog"?

Discontented? Dreaming? Desiring to be someone else? Unhappy with who you are, what you have become? Are you familiar with Psalm 139?

> I praise you because I am fearfully and wonderfully made. Your works are wonderful, I know that full well (Psalm 139:14).

Dream It!

I have not met one woman in my entire life who likes everything about her looks. Do you know that most beautiful women have at least one thing about themselves they detest? Why are we all so hard on ourselves?

We are being brainwashed. Yes, hard-core brainwashing. Who determines what a "10" might be? Beauty is in the eyes of the beholder, if my memory serves correctly.

Each year Oscar awards go to a variety of movies. Look at the enormous diversity in the music we Americans call superb. But when it comes to beauty we have a fixed image in mind. We are programmed to think that image must be seen in our mirror every day. If it isn't, we are losers.

It is difficult to ignore what we see in magazines, on movie screens and what is supported heartily by the media. We are constantly being told who our role model should be.

We must stop at some point and say, "Excuse me, but these models are not my idea of the woman I want to become." Shall we burst the media's bubble by following what the Bible says is true beauty? Most of us are tired of being made to feel small, stupid and simple because we look sort of average and remain faithful to our own husband.

We are women of royal blood, one day heirs to a mansion. Princesses with a power source that New York, Paris or Hollywood cannot comprehend.

Now dream with me for a bit. Without dreaming it, you will never see it.

What is your dream body? Would it be five-feet-eight, with all the parts lookin' great? A Los Angeles psychologist conducted a survey involving more than eight thousand women to determine sexual activity of women who were in a good exercise program. As it turned out, the more sexually responsive women were not those so-called perfect bodies, but were women who were 5' 4 3/4" and weighed 140 pounds.[1]

So apparently the beauty queens do not necessarily take the lead in pleasing their men. What counts is "what you do with what you have."

I would like to challenge you to be the best *you* can. If you need to lose some weight before you feel good about yourself, drop it. Either the weight or the guilt. You cannot convince your husband that you are one delicious dish if you do not believe it yourself.

Have you ever gone to a potluck dinner and someone insists you eat her famous chicken pot pie, but you notice she doesn't have any pot pie on her plate? Do you want to try it? How about the painter who wants to paint your house but you know he hires his own house painted by another company in town? Would you hire someone who tells you, "I'm not very good at this, but I'll sure try"?

It's like the little boy who tried to sell candy bars. His sales pitch began, "These candy bars aren't very fresh, and my doggie was licking the wrapper last night, but my teacher says everyone will probably like them, so my dad says I gotta sell them all." You might buy one because you feel sorry for the little guy, but you probably won't eat it. He did not believe in the product he was selling. He was merely going through the motions because it was required of him.

How many of us go through the motions of making love, feeling all the time like our husbands are just settling for us? You need to see yourself as a prize, someone of great worth. A gift in which your husband should feel proud to indulge. You don't have to be beautiful to accomplish this, but you must feel good about yourself. You and you alone can take your man to ecstasy.

Here are two stories about two very different women. One thought she was wonderfully sexy and used all her stuff to convince her man he was one lucky guy to have her. The other was attractive enough, but *she* did not feel she was.

Sally Secure

Sally is a lady I met who made a lasting impression on me. She was noticeably overweight but dressed like a woman in a fashion magazine. I honestly did not know where she found such wild and wonderful clothing. Her hair and makeup were always just right. And the man who loved her had a great dose of this woman's intoxicating love. She attended all the town activities with "Mr. In-Love" right beside her. It was wonderful to see how he obviously loved her. The extra weight did not hinder her self-image in the least. In her opinion, she was everything any man could want. She told me, "I know I'm not a 10, but my man is sold on me. He has the time of his life with me and there is never a dull moment when I give him my lovin'!"

She explained it this way: "Ever get a fabulous-looking package, the kind that looks like a million bucks? You are so excited and anticipate a gift of rare beauty. But when you open it, there is nothing inside. It's just a beautifully wrapped box. Now which would you rather have? The glitzy box with nothing inside or a plainly wrapped box with a treasured gift enclosed?"

My hat is off to this woman who most definitely knows how to give herself to this lucky guy.

Dianna Defeated

Dianna was at one time a pretty lady. As a young woman she had many male suitors. She fell in love and married one fortunate fellow. She was never more than a few pounds overweight, she had nice curves and wonderful skin, but through the years she began to lose confidence in her attractiveness. Perhaps it was the disappointment of the aging process which gave her the defeated spirit I saw in her eyes.

Regardless of where it started, it was there like a dark cloud everywhere she went. Dianna was so down on herself that being with her for more than a few minutes could leave even the most vivacious personality drooping.

It was worse to see what happened to her husband's attitude toward her.

In the early days he was the most smitten of men. He tried to encourage Dianna, but she was determined that she was worthless.

It was a sad sight the day I saw Dianna's husband carrying his little dog (a Japanese Chin) around from person to person, bragging about how unique this little canine was. This animal was the center of his world. He spoke as if he were carrying a prized possession. He came over to me and began telling me all the talents of ChinChin. I looked over to the farthest corner of the room, and there was Dianna, sitting all alone.

Something was terribly wrong with this picture. How did all of this start? Perhaps in Dianna's very own heart and soul. She did not feel she was worth her husband's attention, and soon he believed it.

Comments That Last a Lifetime

We may have embedded in our minds the faults about our looks or personality which others have pointed out to us unmercifully in our childhood.

Parents do this to their children without realizing the damage being done. The comments of disapproval children hear stay with them for a lifetime. They may receive this message from the time they get up in the morning until they finally get free from the harping by falling asleep at night. Parents want so much for their children to become their best (or, perhaps, *the* best). As adoring parents we want our children to be wonderful, productive adults. We tend to concentrate on correcting all the wrong things we see in them. Yet we fall very short in giving the compliments they deserve.

They hear, "Your hair is a mess. You can't go out like that." "Stand up straight. Do you want to look like Uncle Marvin with a bump on your back?" "You better put that sunscreen on. You know you have terribly sensitive skin." Now this child sees herself as a humped-back, wrinkled-face prune with hair like a wolfman. These negative "uglies" stay in the back of our mind, and are brought to the forefront each time our self-esteem is being challenged.

Sandy With That Horrid Hair!

Sandy's mother has great hair. It is auburn, thick, shiny, naturally curly, perfect hair. Her first-born daughter, Sandy, was born with fine, dull, straight, very unperfect, brown hair.

This mom didn't mean to make Sandy feel that her hair was a disappointment, but she was constantly cutting it—to make it look thicker—and Sandy got her first perm when she was three. You know the old home perm look? She had short, frizzy hair which wasn't the style. Sandy *knew* she had the ugliest hair ever given to a child.

Along with this picture in her mind came another one from friends in school. She was a pitifully skinny kid with long legs. By the age of nine, Sandy could outrun or outclimb any boy. But because she was all legs and a bean pole, she was given the nickname "Spaghetti Legs."

I know worse names have been given, but Sandy truly saw herself as a ugly ragmop. Frizzy hair atop a straight pole is usually not found in the portfolios of great beauties. When Sandy went to a beauty salon, she would inform the stylist that only a miracle could help because she had terrible hair.

Regardless of how many experts tell her she has nice hair, Sandy continues to believe she has the world's worst locks ever to adorn a head.

Compared to women who must overcome great physical handicaps, this is a very small matter. But the thoughts people put into our minds as well as our own self-criticism hinder us from going after things that are within our reach and can destroy our self-image.

So what if we don't have hair like Crystal Gayle or a body like Bo Derek? We are handmade, a perfectly unique image that our heavenly Father crafted Himself. We must dwell on the important fact of who we are becoming every day in Christ Jesus. Whatever hang-ups you have, cut them loose. Choose today to let them go. Like a handful of helium-filled balloons, release your negative thoughts.

Believe It!

If you have a difficult time loving and accepting yourself, you will have a tendency to tear into people whom you feel are superior. Jealousy, the green-eyed monster, will eat you up, destroy you from the inside out. Proverbs 14:30 says: "Envy rots the bones."

Have your bones been hurting lately? Do you ever feel agony deep within when the person you can't stand is getting center stage? Or when your husband has the nerve to compliment her to your face?

Jealousy is a sin that hurts you far worse than it ever hurts the other person. It creates in you a suspicious mind, a negative and critical attitude. For some unknown reason we think that if we want to get ahead we must tear down the person in front of us. But Jesus said in Matthew 20:26-28 that to be great we must be servants; to be first we must be a slave.

I am reminded of a woman who was up for a great promotion. She was certainly the most qualified and seemed the perfect choice. But Jeannie began to think she had to prove she was the best and eliminate anyone who might be competition. She talked openly to the higher-ups in the company of the faults she saw in one person, then another, and another. She began tearing others down to build herself up. Wrong formula.

When the executive board met, they discussed Jeannie's recently discovered personality flaw, gossiping. Since the ability to get along with others was imperative to the position being filled, Jeannie was passed over and the very person she had despised throughout high school and college was chosen.

The only way up is down. It is called humility.

Be a woman who is generous with compliments. If someone is deserving of an encouraging word, say it and mean it. You will begin to feel better about who you are with this simple exercise.

If you believe in yourself, and have a positive image of who you are, you will be much less likely to be jealous of someone else.

See It

Have you heard the slogan Nike uses? "Just Do It." I think that's a great slogan for us to use in this section. We say we want to lose weight, get in shape, improve our wardrobe or get a new look. Why not just do it? We talk and talk, and balk and balk some more, and never get around to it. Come on. Let's just do it.

Skin Care

Heredity, stress, diet and environmental pollution all play a part in determining just how gracefully your skin will age. Doctors and scientists say the sun is the number one culprit, but we have been programmed to think that nothing looks better than a golden-bronzed body. However, these days we are more careful about putting on that tan.

Since the sun and its aging effects can't be completely avoided, you may want to consider using one of the many products designed to keep your skin looking younger: sophisticated moisturizer, Retin-A, collagen creams and collagen injections.

Here are some basics to help us age gracefully:[2]

Teens. Begin to practice good skin care now. When in the sun, *always* use a sunscreen. Try the oil-free type, because your skin is probably producing enough oil naturally. Cleanse your face each morning and night and use a light- to medium-strength astringent. Keep something on your skin for protection against the elements. A slight blush and lipgloss will bring out your youthful beauty.

Twenties. During this time your skin begins to go through changes. Your hormone level is high enough to produce excess oil which causes blemishes from time to time, although they tend to clear up. Pregnancy causes change as well. During the twenties faint wrinkles begin to show up—usually around the eyes.

When exposed to the sun, sunscreen should be worn. It is good to buy foundation with sunscreen in it. Be sure to cleanse skin twice a day, followed by a light astringent. Use a light moisturizer every night. Use foundation and blush to enhance your youthful glow. Apply eye makeup to your taste.

Thirties. This is usually a more stressful time in your life. Juggling children with daily responsibilities can leave little time for a beauty routine, but it is most important not to neglect skin care. The aging process usually starts to show up in your thirties. Skin is slightly dehydrated; cell renewal slows down. Expression lines around eyes, mouth and forehead become more obvious. Moisturizing is no longer an option. Use a very mild cleanser and avoid rubbing or tugging at your skin. Using a damp sponge to apply makeup keeps foundation smooth and natural looking. Use blush and lipstick to add more color. Save the dramatic look for evenings out. *Being consistent* is the key, regardless of which products you choose. According to some experts, being lazy and not cleansing and moisturizing just one night actually adds three more days of aging to your skin.

Forties. By the time most women reach forty, the signs of aging will be more visible. Those tiny wrinkles that have been hanging around are now deepening, and there will be a few new ones. (Oh, thanks a lot, Pam. That really gets me excited about turning forty!) The skin becomes more dehydrated causing dry patches and flaking. That natural color in cheeks and lips has now faded. Supplementary color is most important to add life to that pretty face. At this time in your life, you must have a diligent morning and night skin care program. Products listed as cell renewal help the neck area stay smooth looking. Facials rejuvenate the skin. A light textured foundation in the years after forty is good. Heavy foundation will not cover up wrinkles, but merely enhance their presence. Use a concealer to cover up undereye circles or capillaries which have begun to appear. Apply a soft color to the apples of cheeks and use a matching lipstick.

Fifty Plus. These can be your most exciting years. You have a lot of experience with life, so now you can take it more in stride. Even though skin may have the wrinkles that are inevitable, you now can have a radiance that comes from maturity. Hopefully, you have learned to relax and enjoy life. You have learned to slow down—something the young ones haven't grasped yet.

Get plenty of rest and look your very best by:

- gracing your face with a foundation applied with a sponge;

- adding a softening effect with a blusher applied sparingly;

- using a lip liner filled in with a matching lipstick;

- going very easy on the eye makeup (too much only adds years);

- avoiding heavy, harsh lines of any kind;

- continuing to cleanse and moisturize skin with products specifically designed for your skin type;

- always treating your skin with extreme tenderness.

Beauty Escapes

"Just as you have to let a computer cool down occasionally, the same goes for the human machine. Small cool-downs help prevent meltdown," says Judith Waters, a professor at Fairleigh Dickenson University.[3] We all must spend time pampering ourselves on occasion.

The quick hop in and out of the shower we ritually go through each morning cannot be compared to the relaxation of a hot, bubbly bath. A bath is not just sitting in your own dirty water, as some might mournfully moan. It can be soothing, satisfying, sensual and sumptuous.

Can I tempt you to run to the nearest drug store and load up with wonderful bathing delights such as mineral salts, softening oils, a stimulating body brush, a great magazine or two, and, of course, sparkling cider?

Water has deep relaxing qualities. Whether the crystal tepid bath in the privacy of your own home or a natural mineral-saturated hot springs, your body will respond to the free-moving waves about you. The hustle of the day is washed from your mind and body as you lie back and enjoy the warmth that penetrates deep into your senses.

To get the full treatment of a luxurious bath, you may want to apply a facial mask and deep-condition your hair as well. You must give in completely to the solitude of this moment and refrain from mentally formulating a to-do list or worrying about tomorrow's responsibilities. Make the most of this calming time, and for a nice change, light a candle and play quiet, romantic music. Instructions must be given to all family members that this is a "Do Not Disturb" time for Mom.

Many women have a difficult time being good to themselves, feeling guilty for any personal time they take. But if you make the time to treat yourself to some type of calming experience, you will be far more pleasant to those around you. A rested, refreshing retreat will make you ready to meet the needs of others.

The Bible gives a perfect example of plush indulgence in Esther 2:12:

> Before a girl's turn came to go in to King Xerxes, she had to complete twelve months of beauty treatments prescribed for the women, six months with oil of myrrh and six with perfumes and cosmetics.

I could handle that. How about you?

Diet and Exercise

I read recently of the five age-prone zones.[4] Need I mention them?

1. Drooping bottom
2. Jiggling arms

3. Sagging breasts
4. Rippling thighs
5. Spreading middle

This is not a very encouraging list, but it's honest and truthful. If you suffer from only one of the five, good for you! But for those who have had to spot-exercise for years, this list is all too familiar.

I encourage a simple exercise program you can be consistent with and will find enjoyable. It's not that we have never had an exercise program in our life—the problem comes with *sticking* with one for any length of time. That is why I suggest you find something fun, then you will not dread it. (At least, not as much.)

1. Wonderful Walking
2. Running in rhythm
3. Jogging with Jesus
4. Active aerobics
5. Dancing doubles
6. Swimming swiftly
7. Stately stretches
8. Commercial catch-ups
9. Telephone tummy tucks
10. Thigh thrusts
11. Middle molding

There are many ways to burn off those extra pounds. If you have the time and money, health clubs offer it all: swimming and aerobic classes, spa and sauna, and bikes that work your body to death but take you nowhere.

I prefer to walk—fitness walking to be exact. It

consists of keeping a pretty rigorous pace while walking as if you were following a straight line, one foot in front of the other. Many say that it is the only exercise which can rid the thighs of accumulated cellulite. I usually walk two miles, three to four nights a week. My husband walks with me and we use the time together to discuss the day's events.

Walking is a great way to encourage conversation with your spouse while keeping your heart in good shape and burning extra calories. I usually add some sit-ups and that's my weekly workout.

I'm not the ultra-exercise-buff, as you probably guessed. My friend Nancy, though, is serious. She jogs every morning for an hour or more. She gets ready for the big run by doing stretches and spot exercising those hard-to-get-to muscles. She keeps this program religiously, rain or shine.

You might be in my mode of workout or Nancy's more serious school of fitness. But you should be doing something to keep your body in shape.

Diet

Here are some safe snacks to satisfy your munchies. Each contains approximately one hundred calories per serving:

- sixteen almonds
- one medium apple
- three whole carrots
- eight cashews
- eight saltine crackers
- fourteen cups of lettuce
- four cups of dry popcorn
- eighty-four pretzel sticks
- one hundred forty-three radishes
- seven ounces of apple juice
- sixteen ounces of chicken noodle soup
- seven ounces of low-fat milk
- eighteen ounces of broccoli
- one medium banana
- one brownie
- one and one-half cups cantaloupe

- six and one-half
  tablespoons ice cream
- one-third Snickers candy
  bar

- two cups strawberries
- three-fourths cup nonfat
  yogurt

From this list you can decide if you want 143 radishes or one brownie. However, all calories are not created equal. Now we have information which tells us the fat calorie is much harder to get rid of. In fact, only three calories are used in digesting one hundred calories of fat. The remaining ninety-seven calories turn into body fat. So, you may choose the brownie, but you will have to work extra hard to dispose of it. (A brownie has 40 to 60 percent fat calories.) Vegetables are the superstars when it comes to low-in-fat calories.

Here are some helpful hints for controlling weight:

1. Don't diet. Learn how to cook properly.

2. When you cut back in calories, you also cut out a lot of the taste, smell and texture. If you can't learn to add these qualities back into your diet, you will never keep the weight off.

a. Chocolate syrup has great flavor and has less calories and fat than solid chocolate.

b. Cream soda has a wonderful vanilla flavor with only 100 calories per eight-ounce serving. Our taste buds associate it with eggnog and ice cream and other high-fat foods.

c. Salsa and corn tortillas, toasted to be crisp as corn chips (but no deep-frying), make a low-fat, ultra-high flavor combination.

3. Eat right and change your life, realizing it is a life-long commitment.

4. After losing weight, gradually increase your calorie intake to determine how many calories you can tolerate before you begin to put it back on.[5]

With tongue in cheek, I'll also share these tips to help keep dieting from becoming too stressful:

1. If you drink a diet soda with a candy bar, the calories in the candy bar are cancelled out by the diet soda.

2. When you eat with someone else, if you don't eat more than they do, your calories don't count.

3. Food used for medicinal purposes, such as hot chocolate, toast, Sarah Lee cheesecake, never count.

4. If you fatten up everyone around you, you will look thinner.

5. Movie-related foods, such as Milk Duds, buttered popcorn, Junior Mints, Red Hots and Tootsie Rolls, do not have additional calories because they are part of the entire entertainment package and not part of one's personal fuel.

6. Things licked off knives and spoons have no calories if you are in the process of preparing something. Examples: peanut butter on a knife making a sandwich, and ice cream on a spoon making a sundae.

7. Cookie pieces contain no calories . . . the process of breaking cookies causes calorie leakage.

8. Foods of the same color have the same amount of calories; like spinach and pistachio ice cream, mushrooms and white chocolate.

Why Bother?

Women often tell me, "Pam, my husband loves me just like I am. Why should I go through all this pain and effort to improve?"

I say, "Don't ask your husband to settle for what he's stuck with. Always seek to better your mind and body because you *love him.*"

Jennifer, just a short five years ago, would have said, "My husband loves me just as I am." The problem was what she had become over years of neglect.

Jennifer did not try to update herself as the years drifted by. She wore the same fifties hairstyle. It was quite stylish . . . then. She wore the same style of clothing that her husband thought tantalizing . . . then. Her vocabulary sounded the same because she didn't think it was necessary to get involved with current affairs. After all, she was a homemaker, mother and loving wife. Why bother with all that stuff?

Do you know what happened to this sweet, dear Christian woman who was actually being her *same sweet self?* Her husband was growing and keeping pace with the times. Pretty soon that *sameness* grew very, very boring.

Jennifer's husband came in one day and said, "You bore me to death! Why can't you just update one thing about yourself? I cannot stand this anymore." And off he walked.

This great Christian man whom Jennifer felt so safe and secure with for the past twenty-five years of her life, was now gone.

Emotionally she could not handle this. She took sleeping pills to try to make the pain go away but apparently it wasn't time for her to die just yet.

Instead, Jennifer let a friend help her catch up with the latest fashions and events in the world. It took awhile, but when she met her husband a few months later, she knocked him off his feet with her up-to-date self.

This story has a happy ending, but you and I both know of others which have ended tragically.

Check up on yourself. Are your hair, makeup, clothing and conversation within five years of today's styles? Do not allow yourself to become boring. Keep up on the latest and keep your man going out of his mind, crazy over you.

You cannot get anywhere without a dream, so come on and dream of what you might become. Then *believe* in yourself. As you dream and believe, you will see yourself as someone worthy of your husband's love and attention.

Personal Challenge

1. What is your dream? What goals do you need to set in order to do your very best with what you have? On a piece of paper, list five or more goals.

2. List any negative thoughts you feel have been instilled into your subconscious which hinder the value you have of yourself. After you have written this list on a separate sheet of paper, take it to your heavenly Father and ask Him to remove negative pictures you have of yourself. Then burn the list. Now release them from your mind as you would release a helium-filled balloon. Let them go, never to return to you again.

3. Is there anyone causing you to be a green-eyed monster? Are you eaten up inside with jealousy? Write the name down and confess this sin, vowing to the Lord and yourself to rid your heart and mind of this plague.

4. What plan of attack are you considering to stay in shape physically? *Just do it!*

Understanding your God-given personalities
will help you understand — and appreciate —
each other.

E · I · G · H · T

"So You've Got Personality"!

*O*pposites attract! That's what they say, and it is generally true. A fun-loving party animal will usually marry a well-organized bore. A controlling workaholic will end up with a peaceful, non-aggressive person. Why?

Perhaps we see something in the other person that we lack within ourselves. The playful, free spirit knows he needs someone to get him in shape and keep him on track. Finding this person will give him more time to talk, hop and skip through life while the well-organized one keeps it all together for him. The controlling workaholic doesn't want to be bothered with keeping peace, so the calm and collected spouse is needed to make up for his insensitivity.

We generally do not think about this when we are dating our spouse-to-be. But soon after the wedding bells cease to ring, we realize we are joined with someone completely different from ourselves. Then the fun begins!

Author and speaker Florence Littauer has greatly

expanded on the four basic personality types discovered by Hippocrates: sanguine, choleric, melancholy, and phlegmatic.[1] These words are not new to many of us, but we are going to take a closer look at just how the different personality types affect our marriage relationship.

Florence Littauer, in her book *Personality Plus*, has renamed the four personalities according to the particular trait which is most descriptive. Sanguines have a need to be *popular;* cholerics are *powerful;* melancholies must have things *perfect;* the phlegmatic prefers to have *peace.*

Most of us have one predominant personality type with a second one that influences us as well. On the next few pages I've included Fred and Florence Littauer's "Personality Profile" to help you discover what personality combination you are.[2] Take the time right now to go through this profile, making a list of your strengths and weaknesses. After you've finished, you might try to figure out your husband's personality combination.

DIRECTIONS — In each of the following rows of four words across, place an X in front of the one word that most often applies to you. Continue through all forty lines. Be sure each number is marked. If you are not sure of which word "most applies", ask a spouse or a friend.

STRENGTHS

1	Adventurous	Adaptable	Animated	Analytical
2	Persistent	Playful	Persuasive	Peaceful
3	Submissive	Self-sacrificing	Sociable	Strong-willed
4	Considerate	Controlled	Competitive	Convincing
5	Refreshing	Respectful	Reserved	Resourceful
6	Satisfied	Sensitive	Self-reliant	Spirited
7	Planner	Patient	Positive	Promoter
8	Sure	Spontaneous	Scheduled	Shy
9	Orderly	Obliging	Outspoken	Optimistic
10	Friendly	Faithful	Funny	Forceful
11	Daring	Delightful	Diplomatic	Detailed
12	Cheerful	Consistent	Cultured	Confident
13	Idealistic	Independent	Inoffensive	Inspiring
14	Demonstrative	Decisive	Dry humor	Deep
15	Mediator	Musical	Mover	Mixes easily
16	Thoughtful	Tenacious	Talker	Tolerant
17	Listener	Loyal	Leader	Lively
18	Contented	Chief	Chartmaker	Cute
19	Perfectionist	Pleasant	Productive	Popular
20	Bouncy	Bold	Behaved	Balanced

WEAKNESSES

21	___ Blank	___ Bashful	___ Brassy	___ Bossy
22	___ Undisciplined	___ Unsympathetic	___ Unenthusiastic	___ Unforgiving
23	___ Reticent	___ Resentful	___ Resistant	___ Repetitious
24	___ Fussy	___ Fearful	___ Forgetful	___ Frank
25	___ Impatient	___ Insecure	___ Indecisive	___ Interrupts
26	___ Unpopular	___ Uninvolved	___ Unpredictable	___ Unaffectionate
27	___ Headstrong	___ Haphazard	___ Hard to please	___ Hesitant
28	___ Plain	___ Pessimistic	___ Proud	___ Permissive
29	___ Angered easily	___ Aimless	___ Argumentative	___ Alienated
30	___ Naive	___ Negative attitude	___ Nervy	___ Nonchalant
31	___ Worrier	___ Withdrawn	___ Workaholic	___ Wants credit
32	___ Too sensitive	___ Tactless	___ Timid	___ Talkative
33	___ Doubtful	___ Disorganized	___ Domineering	___ Depressed
34	___ Inconsistent	___ Introvert	___ Intolerant	___ Indifferent
35	___ Messy	___ Moody	___ Mumbles	___ Manipulative
36	___ Slow	___ Stubborn	___ Show-off	___ Skeptical
37	___ Loner	___ Lord over	___ Lazy	___ Loud
38	___ Sluggish	___ Suspicious	___ Short-tempered	___ Scatterbrained
39	___ Revengeful	___ Restless	___ Reluctant	___ Rash
40	___ Compromising	___ Critical	___ Crafty	___ Changeable

NOW TRANSFER ALL YOUR X's TO THE CORRESPONDING WORDS ON THE PERSONALITY SCORING SHEET AND ADD UP YOUR TOTALS.

STRENGTHS

	SANGUINE POPULAR	CHOLERIC POWERFUL	MELANCHOLY PERFECT	PHLEGMATIC PEACEFUL
1	Animated	Adventurous	Analytical	Adaptable
2	Playful	Persuasive	Persistent	Peaceful
3	Sociable	Strong-willed	Self-sacrificing	Submissive
4	Convincing	Competitive	Considerate	Controlled
5	Refreshing	Resourceful	Respectful	Reserved
6	Spirited	Self-reliant	Sensitive	Satisfied
7	Promoter	Positive	Planner	Patient
8	Spontaneous	Sure	Scheduled	Shy
9	Optimistic	Outspoken	Orderly	Obliging
10	Funny	Forceful	Faithful	Friendly
11	Delightful	Daring	Detailed	Diplomatic
12	Cheerful	Confident	Cultured	Consistent
13	Inspiring	Independent	Idealistic	Inoffensive
14	Demonstrative	Decisive	Deep	Dry humor
15	Mixes easily	Mover	Musical	Mediator
16	Talker	Tenacious	Thoughtful	Tolerant
17	Lively	Leader	Loyal	Listener
18	Cute	Chief	Chartmaker	Contented
19	Popular	Productive	Perfectionist	Pleasant
20	Bouncy	Bold	Behaved	Balanced

TOTALS _____

WEAKNESSES

	SANGUINE POPULAR	CHOLERIC POWERFUL	MELANCHOLY PERFECT	PHLEGMATIC PEACEFUL
21	Brassy	Bossy	Bashful	Blank
22	Undisciplined	Unsympathetic	Unforgiving	Unenthusiastic
23	Repetitious	Resistant	Resentful	Reticent
24	Forgetful	Frank	Fussy	Fearful
25	Interrupts	Impatient	Insecure	Indecisive
26	Unpredictable	Unaffectionate	Unpopular	Uninvolved
27	Haphazard	Headstrong	Hard-to-please	Hesitant
28	Permissive	Proud	Pessimistic	Plain
29	Angered easily	Argumentative	Alienated	Aimless
30	Naive	Nervy	Negative attitude	Nonchalant
31	Wants credit	Workaholic	Withdrawn	Worrier
32	Talkative	Tactless	Too sensitive	Timid
33	Disorganized	Domineering	Depressed	Doubtful
34	Inconsistent	Intolerant	Introvert	Indifferent
35	Messy	Manipulative	Moody	Mumbles
36	Show-off	Stubborn	Skeptical	Slow
37	Loud	Lord-over-others	Loner	Lazy
38	Scatterbrained	Short tempered	Suspicious	Sluggish
39	Restless	Rash	Revengeful	Reluctant
40	Changeable	Crafty	Critical	Compromising
TOTALS				
COMBINED TOTALS				

Different Is Not Wrong

Two very different people will not flow together without turbulence from time to time. Knowing which personality you are and identifying that of your husband will help you understand and accept the differences in each other. Most importantly, *different* doesn't mean *wrong*. Sometimes we make the foolish mistake of trying to change the other person into who we are, to make them more acceptable to us. This will only lead to frustration.

Joe met Sandy, a bouncy cheerleader, who was full of life, fun and frivolous talk. She accepted every invitation to any gathering where people would be. He watched her weave her winsome way into each and every heart in the room. He loved her energy. This attracted him since his own introverted personality kept him from going to all of the fun things in school. With Sandy around, he didn't even have to talk. She did enough for both of them.

They had a fabulous fanfare of a wedding, then fled to the quaint cottage Joe had chosen for the honeymoon. Right away Joe began trying to quiet Sandy down. Now that they were adults, certain things would have to shape up in Sandy's life. No more fun. Life had to get serious. Says who? Says Joe!

He spent the next five years organizing, shushing, and lecturing Sandy on how to grow up and lead a peaceful, perfect existence as an adult. Only one problem! Sandy was not a quiet, calm introvert like Joe. Soon the battles began. Sandy continued to go off to parties — alone now, because Joe hated crowds. He despised the way she ignored schedules or kept messy and untidy drawers at home. She seemed so undisciplined.

On the other hand, Joe was boring Sandy to death. He absolutely refused to go to exciting and different places. He was a tightwad, tense and terribly critical. This was not fun anymore.

Joe gave Sandy an ultimatum: "Change your ways or I'm out of here." Sandy gave in to save her marriage. She lived her life Joe's way for fifteen years.

But Sandy was always miserable. She spent each day living a life that wasn't her own. This sent her into a deep depression. One blue Monday morning Sandy took a handful of pills hoping to end her misery.

I lived only a few blocks from Sandy at the time and as I passed by her house her son came running out screaming. Jamie had come home from school to find his mother unconscious. She was barely breathing. The paramedics arrived in time to revive this lady who at one time in her life had been so vivacious.

Joe had literally drained from Sandy her desire for living. He insisted on changing her from the beautiful creation God intended to the creation Joe demanded.

Romans 15:7 says, "Accept one another, just as Christ accepted you." Are you trying to change someone? Make them into another you? Does your marriage really need two of you? The verse in Romans says to *accept* – not rearrange, not fix up, not overhaul, not redesign! *Being different doesn't mean being wrong.*

Blending It Instead of Blowing It

Are you married to a **popular** who is driving you nuts because he loves to be with people? Are you a **powerful** constantly pushing a **peaceful** beyond his limits?

The only person you can change is yourself. Accept and appreciate your spouse for who he is and be willing to make some changes in your life to help him cope with you. Look long and hard at your weaknesses and see how they might irritate and annoy your husband. Here are a few typical examples of problem areas in the personality types.

If you are a **popular**, you'll need to control the chatter once in a while. Give the house some peace and quiet. Learn to put your husband's clothes away in a neat and orderly way. Plan a quiet vacation on occasion and try to enjoy it. Keep the facts as accurate as possible and try to control spending.

Popular Patty always has to be on the phone, on her way out the door or have guests over for dinner. This leaves little time to clean, wash clothes or cook meals. Her household is always in an uproar. This makes her timid, fearing, **peaceful** daughter insecure. It drives her meticulous **perfect** husband right up the wall. Patty needs to make some changes for the sake of the other members in her family. She doesn't need to become a different person, just more sensitive and less selfish.

If you are the **powerful** one, try not to be so bossy, impatient or quick-tempered. You need to let your spouse have his way once in a while. Learn to give compliments in a gracious way. Practice saying, "I'm sorry . . . I was wrong." Realize you don't have to control every situation.

Bob is Mr. Powerful. He runs a giant corporation with many people obeying his every command. When at home he continues to snap out orders. This controlling spirit carries over into many areas of his life. Bob has to control all social activities. He decides *when* everyone will get together, *where* they will get together and *what* the conversation will be while there! This causes people to refuse his invitations (when they have a choice, that is).

If you are the **perfect** personality, you put others at a disadvantage. Whatever the task, or whoever you're with, you will always find imperfections. Stop being so critical and negative as this gets you nowhere. Don't become moody if you haven't checked everything off your list for the day or if some *person* (you could do without most people, anyway) messes up your schedule. Allow for imperfection, especially in yourself.

Priscilla Perfect is well meaning, but she drives her husband crazy, scurrying right behind him, tidying up or redoing the tasks he already did. She warns him constantly of the horrible things that can go wrong in his latest venture as she continues checking off her list of "Things To Do Today." She will sulk for days over something her spouse said and she seems determined to stay in the pit of depression once she's there.

If the personality profile revealed that you are a **peaceful**, you may need to be a little more enthusiastic about life in general. Others must constantly try to get you motivated. You have a lot of fears and one is the fear of *change*. You get in a rut easily, so make an effort to give your husband a little spice once in a while.

Quite often Peggy Peaceful asks me to go shopping with her to help her decide on a new dress. She can't seem to make up her mind on her own. She told me the other day that she wanted to change her furniture around in the living room, but could not decide just how she wanted it. I asked her how long the furniture had been arranged like it is now. She said, "Oh, I don't know. Probably around twelve years or so." Peggy needs to dare to be different and do it without delay.

Emotional Needs — Enough to Go Around

We all have very different emotional needs. We probably have no idea how to meet the needs of our spouses, so we usually end up giving *them* what *we* need emotionally, thinking they are quite happy with that.

I am a **popular** and my husband Richard is a **perfect/powerful.** When we got married at ages eighteen and twenty, we had no idea we were so different. We struggled to meet each other's emotional needs.

One of the ways we failed was on birthdays. Every year I, the **popular**, would plan the biggest blowout of the decade for Richard, my **perfect/powerful** husband.

I would have balloons in every shape and size, loud music, tons of food and of course, lots and lots of people. What person in his right mind would not love a rollicking birthday like the ones I could put together?

That's right, a **perfect**. So Richard, in great pain, would smile faintly through the ordeal as I laughed gaily and entertained our guests. (Someone had to, since the guest of honor was being most ungrateful for all the work I had gone to just for him.) I would end up crying because he didn't have a good time, and he would be hurt that I could not understand his needs.

Then came June 24th every year, my birthday. I would grow more excited as each day passed in June, knowing that soon it would be my birthday. This was the day I was to be spoiled, surprised and surrounded by all the hundreds of people who loved me.

I was surprised all right. There was never any big surprise and certainly no people. Just a quiet dinner for two in a nice restaurant with a practical gift that came with a guarantee.

I cried every birthday for ten years. Why, oh why, couldn't Richard plan just one fabulous birthday?

Why? Because he was giving me the kind of birthday *he* wanted every year. It took us a while to catch on, but now we're pretty good at planning the perfect birthday for each other.

Richard turned forty this year. For several years I had done the dinner for two, and for a party-lover like me that is difficult. I had already kidnapped him a few years back. Yet, I did want to make this fortieth birthday somewhat memorable. I had a plan.

I told Richard I would like to pick him up for lunch on his birthday. I said I would arrive at his office at noon. I also phoned his secretary and told her to cancel all his appointments for the rest of that afternoon, as he would not be returning to work after lunch.

I did arrive at noon as I said, but I was in a limousine instead of the family wagon. The driver knocked on Richard's office door, greeted him, rolled out the red carpet, gave him a red rose and told him his limo was waiting.

Richard, completely dumbfounded by now, followed the driver out to the limo, wondering what was going on. When the driver opened the door, there I was, all decked out in an evening dress that would knock your socks off.

"Ready for lunch, dear?" I said. We had an elegantly catered lunch served on silver trays. The white-gloved limo driver poured sparkling cider into chilled crystal goblets. Ripe juicy strawberries with light, fluffy whipped cream completed the menu.

The chauffeur took us for a quiet drive in the foothills as we listened to Richard's favorite music and enjoyed our fancy gourmet meal . . . just the two of us. At the end of the romantic drive, the limo left us at a quaint motel in a small town where no one could find us.

This was the most perfect birthday I could ever plan for my **perfect/powerful** husband. Just Richard and me, alone in the serenity of love.

We both know what the other one needs now, and rarely is it that which *we* would choose for ourselves. We have discovered that being different is not wrong.

So You're Not the Perfect Match?

Communication patterns for varied combinations of **popular**, **powerful**, **peaceful** and **perfect** will vary. Below I've given some tips to help you and your mate work together despite your differences. Find your personality trait, then look for your mate's.

If you are the **powerful** and your husband is

- **popular**, you need to:

    Reduce emphasis on results. Learn to compliment and praise him publicly. Increase your ability to laugh and have a good time.

- **peaceful**, you need to:

    Take time to listen to him. You must give him the opportunity to prove his self-worth, *his* way. Refrain from pushing too hard. Give him the place of authority in your home.

- **powerful**, you need to:

    Allow your husband his area of authority and stay out of his territory. If he doesn't ask for advice, keep it to yourself. Don't play tug of war for power. Learn to give him a lot of appreciation for his accomplishments.

- **perfect**, you need to:

    Slow down and pay more attention to details. He wants to be thorough in situations. Allow him this right. Learn to be more sensitive to his emotions. Give him space to be left alone from time to time.

If you are the **popular** and your husband is

- **powerful**, you need to:

    Work harder for results. Be sure to follow

through. Be sincere when giving praise. He needs to know you really *are* impressed with his work.

● **popular**, you need to:

Stop grandstanding and calling so much attention to yourself. Allow him to be the life of the party too. Make big efforts to compliment and praise him publicly in every area of life.

● **peaceful**, you need to:

Stop dragging him to every party in town. Understand that he will never show emotions as much as you, so stop being disappointed. Think of ways to encourage his dry sense of humor. Rest in the quiet he can bring to your life.

● **perfect**, you need to:

Be more exact and think about what you are saying. Be tidier, thrifty and respect his lists of "to do's." Do not joke when he is hurting. A joke will only make the hurt worse.

If you are **peaceful** and your husband is

● **powerful**, you need to:

Stop rambling and say what you mean. Stand up for yourself. He needs for you to be strong or he will walk all over you. Make a decision and stick with it.

● **popular**, you need to:

Add some spice to your life. You will grow very boring if you do not make this effort. Go with him to most of his fun things. Don't be content to send him out alone. Speed up some.

● **perfect**, you need to:

Make rational choices *on your own*. Be the aggressive one on occasion. If you aren't watchful, this marriage will become very dull and clinical.

● **peaceful** you need to:

Get motivated and help your husband realize his potential as well. He needs to feel he's worth something—help him see that he is. Make a big effort to talk and share with him.

If you are **perfect** and your husband is

● **powerful**, you need to:

Cut all the details and give him straight answers. Allow him the right to do his job his way, even if it isn't perfect. Learn to give him appreciation without a negative footnote added.

● **popular**, you need to:

Learn to relax and laugh when he's telling a not-so-factual story. He needs to hear a lot of praise from you in his success. Do not critique him to death.

● **peaceful**, you need to:

Strive for openness. Allow him time to make decisions. Watch that you don't organize the life out of your marriage. Respect his true fears.

● **perfect**, you need to:

Watch that your marriage doesn't become a contest of trying to out-chart and out-list each other. Try being spontaneous from time to time. Do not let your marriage become too predictable. Enjoy those long, meaningful talks you can have together.

Sexuality by Personality

Each of the four personality types respond in their own way to intimacy. Each will vary due to past influences.

If home life was not good for you or your spouse or perhaps the model you had to observe was warped, or if there was abuse of some type, your personality's natural sexual response could be suppressed. If you or your husband are experiencing serious sexual problems, you need to talk it through and perhaps seek professional help.

A **popular** usually wants lovemaking to be fun! He will want variety, so make sure you give it to him. The **popular** can have a real problem with being faithful, because he loves attention from someone new. Give him a lot of attention and variety. Spontaneity is supreme. Forget the formula and get on with the fun and the grand finale.

The **perfect**, on the other hand, will tend to "do it by the book." He loves music and atmosphere. Making love is very serious business to the **perfect**. So is commitment. He would think it through very carefully before he would ever stray.

A **powerful** will want to be in control, deciding when, where and how you will make love. He is more interested in the results than how he goes about it. He may even seem regimental at times. **Powerfuls** are generally people of great passions.

The **peaceful** wants very much to please his lover, but will have a difficult time deciding just how that might be done and then doing it. He will most certainly need someone to be aggressive and get things going, but once begun he aims to please. He would never hurry through this special time, and would give you all the time needed.

I have friends who have been married sixteen years. Recently, things had been going very poorly in their marriage. He was constantly upset and disappointed in her, and she was miserable for letting him down. They were totally unaware of what the other needed emotionally. I recommended that they read together Florence Littauer's two books, *Personality Plus* and *Your Personality Tree*. They spent an entire weekend absorbed in these books.

I received a call the next week from the woman and she was singing a brand new song of love. She said, "Pam, reading those books opened up a new world to us. We are closer than we ever thought possible, and a new love is taking shape in our hearts. Thank you! Thank Florence for us! We will never be the same because of what she revealed in her books on personalities."

I highly recommend these two books. Much of my research on this subject has come from Florence's wisdom which I gleaned from her lectures as well as *Personality Plus* and *Your Personality Tree*. You can find these in your local Christian bookstore.

Personal Challenge

1. First determine what your main temperament is. Then have your husband do the same.

2. Write down on a piece of paper the weaknesses you are aware of in yourself.

3. Now go back to each weakness and decide what you can do to keep this weakness from becoming a source of irritation to your husband.

4. This is a great time to find out from your husband if you have been meeting his emotional needs. Have you been giving to him what you have been needing from him? (Remember my birthday parties?) Ask him tonight.

5. The most beautiful discovery in all of this information is that *different* doesn't mean *wrong*. Look at your husband's differences and repeat several times, *Different doesn't mean he is wrong.* Allow him that right.

*If you do not enjoy intimacy
it could be because of some unresolved pain
in your past.*

N · I · N · E

To "Dream, Dream, Dream" Is Not Always So Wonderful

At this point, some of you may be saying, "Pam, I really like your ideas. I agree that I should be my husband's mistress. I want to do all the things you suggest, but when it comes to lovemaking sometimes I just freeze. My heart wants to respond, but my mind and body refuse to cooperate."

If you have come from an abusive background, you may be feeling that way. Please don't be discouraged and give up on the possibility of having a satisfactory love life. In spite of a dysfunctional background, your desires can still be fulfilled as long as you are willing to face the past, get the emotional help you need, and place your response in God's hands.

If a past experience or relationship haunts you so that you cannot fully enjoy intimacy with your husband, let me suggest that you read *Freeing Your Mind From Memories That Bind* by Fred and Florence Littauer. Then ask the Lord if you should seek professional help. All the suggestions in the world are not going to improve your love life if you do not acknowledge and deal with your damaged past.

I have two friends who were both diagnosed with breast cancer. From the first day, my friend Penny wanted to know what she could do to help the treatment be successful. She read everything she could get her hands on. She changed her diet, took special vitamins and followed the doctor's orders to a tee.

The single most important thing that Penny did was admit, *I really do have cancer.* As this dreaded disease smashed straight into her life, she knew her future full of dreams would be short-lived unless the battle taking place within her body could be won.

It was a battle! She suffered and shuddered in despair. She sank into depression over the way her body was ravaged by the disease. She swore she could not live through another treatment. But as Penny allowed the pain of healing to take place in her life, she began to win the battle over the cancer. Soon the ordeal was over. She was whole again.

My other friend Teresa, diagnosed with the same type of cancer, refused to let the disease be taken from her body. She played at obeying the doctor. She ignored the cancer's deadly power.

Teresa had watched people go through the horrible treatment. She decided, "I'll take my chances on fighting it myself."

Many people tried to reason with her about the incredible foolishness of this decision, but she was determined to keep this horrid enemy within. She trusted it to stay put and not take over her body. But cancer is not a friend to be trusted. Soon it had taken Teresa's body captive. She lived a short six months. Refusal to admit the truth cost Teresa her life.

If you have unresolved hurts in your past, admitting that you have emotional damage and then seeking help are important first steps to take. Another step in the healing process involves the willingness to forgive those who have hurt you so deeply.

Forgive and Live

Hate, refusing to forgive, holding on to hurt, is like allowing a cancerous tumor to remain in your body. It will not stay put. Soon your entire body will be infected with hate and anger. The hurt will fester and begin to ooze infectious venom. As you speak, your words will convey the hate that lies within your soul. Everywhere you look, you will see infuriating situations. Your mind will be filled with suspicion and stress. The disease will grow deeper and deeper into your personality. Soon you will be eaten up with hate, anger, and an unforgiving heart.

There are hundreds of thousands of hurting people in our world. If I could avenge their hurts, if I could make things right for them, if I had the power to correct all the injustices done to the innocent, I would. You would too. But sin is here. The prince of sin lives among us. People like you and me suffer because of sin in this wicked world of ours.

A friend of mine and her two children were recently murdered in their home. We had laughed and played together as carefree teenagers. Now she is gone. Only Jesus

Himself can comfort the pain her family is suffering.

Her family will have to, at some point, deal with forgiveness. As unjust as this crime was, not to forgive only allows the hurt to grow day after day after day. The hate will soon consume them, corrupt their peace, and control their lives.

Help! I'm Hurting

Hurts that are not as extreme as murder or victimization can still eat away at our peace and cause us pain. Perhaps someone lied about you, misunderstood you, deserted you, betrayed your love. Maybe that hurt was deep and devastating and you still have the raging disease of unforgiveness in your body.

Whatever the offense, slight or enormous, it has to go. Right now. The healing process needs to begin today.

Authors Maxine Hancock and Karen Burton Mains write:

> Forgiveness is laying down a ten-pound load of pain strapped to your chest which you have carried to bed, through each day, to work, into all your relationships. You put it down, truly lay it aside when you forgive.[1]

To forgive does not mean to condone. It is not saying, "What you did was right. What you did was okay." It is deliberately choosing to stop the pursuit of vindicating your hatred. It is turning the judgment and punishment over to God, the higher authority.

The word *forgive* comes from an ancient word meaning "to give away." It means saying, "Father, their punishment is in Your hands. I give You the hate and anger I feel toward them. I let go of it all."

Supernatural Love

I know of a happily married couple who were very close and very much in love. When people saw them together they knew it was a tremendous marriage.

One day the husband's company notified him that he would need to work away from home for three months. He was not given an option. If he wanted to remain employed by this firm, he had to take the assignment. The separation was not something they looked forward to, but they both knew they could manage for three months.

The sad day of his departure came. Both pledged their love and promised to write daily. So began the three-month separation.

Days went by, and in the beginning letters were exchanged regularly. But as weeks passed, the husband began to slack off in his letter writing. Soon he wrote one letter every couple of weeks. Then they came even farther apart.

Finally he was due to come home. But a letter came saying he had to stay longer than expected. The weeks turned into months, the month into an entire year. The faithful, loving wife waited for the day when they could once again be together.

One morning she opened the mailbox, and there was a letter from her husband. Excited as always and filled with anticipation that he had finally been given the okay to come home, she opened it. As she began reading the scribbled words, she saw right away that this letter was different from the others. It was a letter of confession. He had found someone else to love—a very young and beautiful girl.

The news sent her into bitter agony. It took time to let go and work through the anger, resentment, wrath and fury.

But she was brave. She chose to let God deal with her husband and his sin. She forgave him and his young bride. She even wrote to them on occasion, sending her love and prayers for their happiness. An incredible healing had taken place in her heart.

Several years passed, and one day a letter came from the young bride, now a mother with two babies. Her husband had died from cancer, leaving the three of them penniless.

To rejoice at this point and say, "Finally, they got theirs," would be the natural response of someone holding on to hatred and hurt. But this was not the woman's response at all.

She immediately wired money for three plane tickets along with a message: "Come and bring the children to my home. With God's help we will raise the babies together."

Incredible? Unnatural? Yes, it was superhuman — the supernatural way to respond, God's grace alone.

This woman had felt the pain of rejection, the powerful urge to get revenge, the poison of hate, the pangs of loneliness, the paralyzing hurt of humiliation. She had all the feelings of anger ever experienced in human flesh. But she had to make a choice. A choice to forgive these two people and get on with her life or to become a bitter old woman at the age of thirty-five. She, fortunately, chose not to become the bitter old woman.[2]

Bitter or Better?

What are your choices today? Are you holding on to a festering hurt? Are you raging inside with hate and anger? If you are, chances are you are becoming a bitter old woman, even if you are only twenty years old.

One little boy described forgiveness as the perfume

a flower gives out after it's stepped on. Have you been stepped on? What perfume are you giving out?

Forgiving your offender will release you. As you willfully decide it is over, day by day you will remember less and less of the pain. Make the choice to forgive. Let the healing begin.

Forgiving, Not Forgetting

As long as you are of sound mind you probably won't be able to forget what caused your pain. To erase something from the human computer is almost impossible. Once an image is in the brain, it can be called back to the main screen at the command of the will. This is the way we are put together. But you can do something to control this powerful computer.

Don't View the Reruns

Many people recall and replay the offense over and over in their mind. They say, "I have given it to the Lord to work out," but they continue to relive the pain again and again with their very own built-in video player. Details of the act and conversation are watched repeatedly, each time growing larger, more intense. In fact, the mind may even embellish the offense to include more details than the original act.

Refusing to watch this video replay when the mind brings these pictures into view is precisely the way to keep the images from coming back. Do not allow reruns to bring back the original hurt, pain and anger.

Of course, the reruns will continue to show up on the screen from time to time—when you hear a certain song, drive by a special place, see that familiar face or hear a particular name. At that point you have a choice. You can watch the rerun and relive the pain, or you can switch channels, refusing to dwell on the past. The choice is yours.

Flourishing Despite the Pain

Pain from the past is ever-present in all of us. I can still vividly remember being hurt deeply as a six-year-old girl.

Bubble Gum Blues

When I was in the first grade, my father changed pastorates. We moved to a different town, and suddenly I was the new kid in school. I felt plenty insecure about not having friends there. I can remember the gnawing pain of loneliness when I arrived at the new school. Each morning as my dad dropped me off in front of the mammoth, red brick building, big tears welled up in my scared brown eyes.

I tried very hard to fit in and meet a few friends, but it was not an easy job. I did everything I knew to do. Finally, a gesture of friendship came. Two girls in my class offered me a piece of purple bubble gum. I was thrilled at this token of friendship. I unwrapped it carefully, put it in my mouth, and began chewing. I kept it all recess and when the bell rang to return to class, I forgot to remove it.

I sat at my desk looking straight into my teacher's eyes. My hands were folded, just as they were to be, during our reading time. As she peered down on the thirty-one six-year-olds in their assigned seats, I noticed her eyes stopped when she came to me.

She had observed the purple glob in my mouth.

"Pamala Condit! Come up to the front of the room," she ordered.

Stunned, I rose from my desk and reluctantly walked to the front of the classroom.

"Students," she began, "do we have class rules?"

"Yes, Mrs. Ardgrave," they answered.

"Pamala has broken one of our rules today. She is very, very bad. She must remember never to break this rule again." By now, tears were running down my freckled face. "Give me the gum," she ordered.

I took the gum from my mouth and placed it in her hand. She then turned me around to face the class and put the purple glob of gum on the tip of my nose.

"Students who break class rules are very foolish. Pamala is foolish today."

At that, she quickly turned on her heels and walked from the room, leaving me standing there to face a most unmerciful multitude of six-year-olds. They pointed, jeered and laughed. Their cruelty was at the expense of my self-image. I was a new girl in school, only trying to get someone to be my friend.

This incident stayed with me for many years. Each time I was asked to get up in front of a group of people, I imagined they were laughing at me — that I still had purple bubble gum on my nose.

How ironic that the Lord would eventually call me to speak to large groups of people. I have chosen to forgive the teacher and the students. I am the one who has benefited from this. I no longer break out in a cold sweat or get nauseous when asked to speak in public. It was not easy to release those feelings, but I did.

Replace the Bad Dream With a Good One

Many women have told me they have a difficult time letting go of guilty feelings from the past. Perhaps you were promiscuous as a teenager or single adult, and now you are bringing guilt feelings into your marriage bed.

Many things initiated those bad feelings in Kim. She

told me, "Every time Paul starts to get intimate, a horrible feeling pours over me. I freeze up. The way he kisses me, where he touches me, the words he uses—all bring back a bad video replay to my mind."

Many women like Kim have a past that continues to haunt them. The guilt they had as teens, sneaking behind their parents' backs, sleeping with the boys who asked, is still affecting their lives today.

As the Lord forgives us, He also wants us to forgive ourselves: "Therefore, there is now no condemnation for those who are in Christ Jesus, because through Christ Jesus the law of the Spirit of life set me free" (Romans 8:1, NIV). If you are a Christian, you are set free. Let the guilt be replaced by freedom—freedom which allows you to love and enjoy your husband.

One tactic Satan uses is self-punishment. He comes to you again and again, reminding you of just how terrible you are. The only way to get rid of him is to say once and for all, "Yes, I did those things. But they have been confessed and I am completely forgiven. So, get out of here. You cannot bring them up to me anymore. The Lord chooses not to remember them, and neither do I." Say this every time Satan tries to ambush you. He will soon know that won't work on you anymore.

If a scene that you have tried to forget continues to come back on the screen of your mind, you need to replace it with another picture. Do not let it replay over and over. This only drives it deeper into your subconscious. Find a good picture and lay it over the top of the ugly scene you wish to blot out. Do this until the bad scene is completely faded.

It is totally up to you. Keeping the destructive disease of unforgiveness within your body will eventually destroy you. The better choice is to forgive.

As you deal with the pains of your past and progress to a point of forgiveness, you will be released into the freedom of loving. Let go of the hurt. This will mean new life to you and your marriage. Choose today to live.

Personal Challenge

1. Dig into your inner being to see why you are uncomfortable about certain things. Uncover the past so you can begin to heal.

2. Find a special somebody you can trust and talk out your feelings. Letting the words come out is a release. A mistake some people make is to never face the hurt, to cover it up. You need to get it out in the open and face it. You may even need a professional Christian counselor. (Be very cautious when choosing a counselor. Get recommendations from people you trust.)

3. Tears can be the healing balm you need. Go ahead and let it all out. Cry, pray, release. Allow your heart to be freed from past hurts.

4. List on a piece of paper any offenses that you still hold in your heart, things which you have refused to forgive. Take each one separately and pray, "Father, I want to forgive this offense. Help me to do that right now." Go through each offense in detail, forgiving every single bit of hurt. Release even the slightest amount of anger. Pray until it is gone. If you have a difficult time doing this, I recommend you contact Philippian Ministries (8515 Greenville Ave., #N203, Dallas, TX 75243), a group which helps hurting men and women pray for emotional healing through forgiving prayer. They can help you locate the ministry nearest you.

5. Practice letting go of hurt, anger and hate this week when an offense is made. Learn this process of letting go in everyday life.

T · E · N

So You Didn't Marry "Johnny Angel"

Your husband may have the desire to completely fulfill your needs in the romance department, but perhaps he just doesn't know how. Maybe his parents never modeled a loving relationship. It is very difficult to build a wonderful relationship without observing it in someone else. Many men simply act out what they witnessed day after day in their homes. They haven't the slightest idea of how to show the love and emotion they truly feel. They are romance illiterates.

The "Would Be" Johnny Angel

But all is not lost! Provided with non-threatening information and given time, these men can become wonderful lovers. Attacking them with, "Why aren't you like Patty's husband?" or "You just can't meet my needs," will only discourage them. They need some instruction on the subject. You can help them get that information.

A few helpful hints:

Go on a retreat that focuses on the needs of couples. Retreats provide opportunities to talk about weaknesses in both partners. It can be a time for your husband to see other men who struggle but are willing to change. And it isn't a surprise attack. Both of you know it is a couple's retreat, so you expect to talk about things related to marriage.

Good books can be eye-openers for the man willing to read. I suggest: *ManTalk* by Dan Benson; *If Only He Knew* by Gary Smalley; *What Wives Wish Their Husbands Knew About Women* by James Dobson.

Be very careful when suggesting that your husband read one of these books. He may take it as a put-down. Be diplomatic. Allow him the choice to read or not to read. Talk about it *before* you run down to the bookstore and buy him a copy.

Take a look at who his male companions are. How do these men treat their wives? Are they a positive influence on him?

Find a couple in which the husband treats his wife with love and respect, and make opportunities to be with that couple socially. The more your husband sees respect and romance acted out, the more he will be aware of his own shortcomings and how he can improve. Warning: Bragging about this "ideal" marriage too much will cause him to resent the other couple. Your husband is capable of observing without a sideline coach.

Perhaps your husband does not feel the freedom to love you the way you desire because of something buried deep within him. There could be an emotional block, something he may not even be aware of. Even if he denies anything being wrong, he could be influenced by that hidden ghost.

My friend Sarah came to me last year feeling terribly frustrated about her physical relationship with her husband. I listened as she wept and poured out the fact that her husband Tom had made love to her only a few times during their eight years of marriage. She felt like a real failure, a total turnoff. After all, her husband was a healthy, red-blooded American male. Why wasn't he responding to his pretty, sexually aggressive wife? He made her feel cheap and dirty for having this "distasteful" desire.

I listened to her tell me of all the wonderfully creative ways in which she had approached her husband. She tried it all. I suppose she could write her own book on how to set the mood. The book would not have a very happy ending, though. Time after time she was turned away. Regardless of her endless lists of romantic ideas, none of them could lure her man into bed with her.

In her own eyes Sarah felt like a complete failure. But I saw her quite differently. She had stayed with her husband for eight years, even though she was frantic with the situation. Sarah was still trying to make it work. It was evident she was very much in love with Tom. She even made excuses for his cold responses toward her. Sarah was not a failure. She was spectacular.

After listening to her I asked if perhaps there might be something in Tom's past which would make him dislike sex. Maybe it was an immoral parent who had been open and crass concerning sexual matters. Or perhaps he himself had a past of sexual perversion and was trying to forget it. Though Tom had never revealed anything, Sarah decided to talk with him and see if it was a possibility.

She called long distance late one Saturday night, crying. I could barely understand her words, but I could tell her tears were tears of joy and relief. She told me Tom had finally confessed his deep, dark secret. It was true. He had been tormented over something in his past.

As a teenager Tom had had sex with any and every girl who said yes. After Tom changed his ways, settled down and married, the guilt of his past made him detest sex. He did not even realize he was letting his past possess him in this way.

Tom began to see a Christian counselor and they worked through the guilt. Tom finally admitted his problem, which had nothing to do with his wife after all. If they had not uncovered the cause of Tom's problem, Sarah would have continued to feel like a failure.

Tom was a Johnny Angel in the end. He just had to get well first.

The "Could Be" Johnny Angel

There are certainly those men who could be dream lovers, the ideal Johnny Angels, but they just need some time. Actually, both partners need time. Many women come into marriage with Cinderella dreams. They read about great marriages, see them in others and expect theirs to be perfect from day one.

The truth is, some couples will have to work much harder to create a spectacular marriage. While some seem to just click from the word "go," others will take longer to develop the same oneness, the same level of communication, as the perfect match. Why?

I formulated a theory. This comes from many years of working with couples and investigating the reason behind problems that seem to develop in marriage.

Theory: Couples who have

- known each other for two years or longer,

- come from similar family backgrounds, and
- developed the *same* commitment to Christ,

will have far less problem areas to work through than those who do not have these same things going for them.

Do Not Rush Into Marriage. Take time to really know the person you'll be spending your life with.

Marsha and Phillip were both raised on the West Coast by parents who were upper middle class. Both of their fathers worked while their mothers chose to stay home and be full-time homemakers. Marsha and Phillip both had a deep commitment to Christ. They understood where the other one was coming from because they had been raised pretty much the same way.

Marsha had known Phillip for several years and had seen how he responded in various circumstances before they actually started dating. She had a better handle on the real Phillip. Anyone can camouflage his or her real self for a year, but it is difficult to hide the real person for two years or longer.

Some might ask, "What if we don't have any of the above going for us?"

You'll have to work harder, wait patiently, and be willing to blend together. Above all, give each other the right to a different opinion.

Family Background. The woman raised with very little material wealth who marries a rich kid will probably be frustrated on more than one occasion. Each has an entirely different concept of money, where it comes from and how to spend it.

Blake was a Big Man on Campus. He drove a hot-looking sports car and looked like a dream. When he walked across the university campus, every girl took notice. Who ever imagined he would fall for Miss Nobody from a small

Midwest town? But it happened. He just had to have this soft, innocent beauty for his bride.

But when it came to money matters, they discovered they were worlds apart. Blake had never been to a blue light special at K mart, and his blushing bride had certainly never shopped Macy's White Flower Day. She always wanted to buy the least expensive product, while Blake looked for craftsmanship and quality.

Neither of them were wrong in their convictions. But they had to sit down and talk. They realized there had to be compromise. They found there were advantages in shopping both the discount and the finer department stores. But in their first few years of marriage this difference in family background caused some major arguments.

Spiritual Commitment. The woman who committed her life to the Lord at an early age and was raised attending church will find many frustrations if she marries a man who has little interest in spiritual things. It may seem like an unimportant issue while dating, but scores of married women attend church alone week after week because of this difference. Even if the husband decides he would like a Christian marriage, the woman raised in the Bible will be spiritually ahead of him for a long while. Remember this and be patient.

When there are major difference in these areas of your lives, you will have to roll up your sleeves and work hard. It will take longer to produce peaceful harmony in your marriage relationship. But it is possible—no doubt about it. Given some time, your husband may be the "could be" Johnny Angel.

The "Never Will Be" Johnny Angel

Love is a choice. Initiating love, accepting love and

giving love are the actions of a willing individual. Sometimes a man, for whatever reasons, chooses not to demonstrate love to his wife. And his wife's actions may have little influence on his decision.

In my early days of marriage I worked for a businessman who had a lovely wife. She loved him dearly. She always looked great and took excellent care of their children and fabulous home. She constantly did thoughtfully romantic things for him. Yet, he chose to have several girlfriends on the line at the same time. Many were his business trips out of town with other women.

Why would a man do this to such a great wife? He chose to. This man lived a selfish life. I know it was a miserable situation for his wife, yet she loved him.

"I'm committed to this marriage," she told me one afternoon. And she was. For years she tried everything to make it work, but he refused to respond. He chose not to love or be loved by his wife. He eventually chose to divorce her. These were his choices. At least the wife knew in her heart she had given it her best. She was not haunted by guilt due to neglect. She had no regrets. It was his own choice to refuse her love.

Be certain to give 100 percent in your marriage relationship. But remember, if Johnny absolutely refuses to be Johnny Angel and insists on being Devilish Dan, that is his choice. Don't punish yourself for his selfishness. And please, if you find yourself in an emotionally or physically abusive relationship, seek help from your pastor or a Christian counselor.

Don't Give Up Too Soon

Be gentle with your husband as you put forth the extra effort to make your relationship better. This book cannot guarantee that your husband will respond ecstatically to your new ideas. People seldom change overnight, and your Johnny Angel may take a long time to respond. You need to work at these ideas for a lifetime. Don't give up too soon. You may be one day short of victory. Keep on going!

When things go wrong, as they sometimes will,
When the road you're trudging seems all up hill,
When the funds are low and debts are high,
And you want to smile, but you have to sigh,
When care is pressing you down a bit,
Rest, if you must, but don't you quit.

Life is queer with its twists and turns,
As every one of us sometimes learns,
And many a failure turns about
When he might have won had he stuck it out.
Don't give up, though the pace seems slow —
You might succeed with another blow.

Often the goal is nearer than
It seems to a faint and faltering man.
Often the struggler has given up
When he might have captured the victor's cup.
And he learned too late, when the night slipped down,
How close he was to the golden crown.

Success is failure turned inside out —
The silver tint of the clouds of doubt.
And you never can tell how close you are,
It may be near when it seems afar.
So stick to the fight when you're hardest hit —
It's when things seem worst that you mustn't quit.

Personal Challenge

1. Perhaps your husband is a "Would Be" Johnny Angel if given the information and encouragement he needs. Choose one or more of the helpful hints on page 126 and go to work on them today.

2. Have you inadvertently pushed your husband away by comparing him to someone else's husband? Confess this to him and vow to refrain from it from now on.

3. In light of the theory on page 128, are the expectations you have of your marriage realistic? Go over each ingredient, writing beside it your own personal data. This will show you areas you might need to work on.

4. Have you given 100 percent to a marriage in which your spouse seems to have no concern or commitment? Keep giving it your best, but also remember that he, too, must choose. Do not go through this frustration without help. Call your pastor or Christian counselor today.

5. This book is not one you read once and set aside. Remember to keep it handy to reread when you feel yourself growing neglectful. Love and marriage is the work of a lifetime. Keep this book in plain sight as a reminder to continue doing the special things that will help keep the romance alive.

E · L · E · V · E · N

Is "Everybody Somebody's Fool"?

*I*t has been said, "The person who commits adultery doesn't just get up one morning and decide to have an affair." We do not plan for such calamity—it usually hits when we least expect it. It is like a tornado. The storm begins ever so softly . . . everyone unaware of the forceful wind accumulating in the center of the unnoticed funnel. Little by little this breeze builds. It grows stronger into a fierce giant, carrying with it complete destruction for everyone and everything in its path. Plowing through, tearing apart, uprooting, wrecking even the most secure-looking homes.

Unguarded Places

King David is a sobering reminder of the realities of adultery, a true story of undenied desire with a dreadful finale. David was in an unguarded place—on his rooftop, all alone. What was he doing up there, anyway? Relaxing? Daydreaming? Putting his nose into his neighbor's business? In any case, he was in an unguarded place, one set up by Satan himself. David could argue that his rooftop was a safe enough place to be, but not that day. It may have been an all-right place, but it was definitely the wrong time to be there.

My confession to a close call comes most humbly. I can tell you it was all very innocent . . . at least in the beginning.

Each morning at precisely 8:25 A.M., I would walk my very scared and reluctant kindergartner from our car to her classroom. We faced this routine each day, going through the same reassuring gestures: a big hug, a confident smile and a firm handshake. All to convince my scared little kitten that "Mommy will return."

I wasn't alone in this ritual. In the beginning, there were many shaky legs and teary-eyed five-year-olds facing a terrifying three hours. One by one these children grew braver and soon the group had diminished to a crowd of two — my Amy and a towhead of a little guy, Jeffy.

Jeffy was escorted to class each morning by his Sachs-Fifth-Avenue-looking father. You know the type: square jaw, designer suits, and a perfect smile that would cut through any heart in a flash.

As it happened, Jeffy's father and I found ourselves walking to our cars together day after day. From the very start, I was aware of his cordial attitude toward Amy as well as his attentiveness to me. We chatted very briefly at first. It wasn't long until the small talk grew into full-grown conversations. Was he likable? Yes. Handsome? For sure. Wooing? Most definitely!

I admit I began to feel uneasy. But as is common, I convinced myself we were not doing anything wrong. Each time we spoke, my feelings of guilt weakened.

I enjoyed his friendship, this new attention, the

secret feelings. I told myself again and again, "This is only a friendship; nothing is going on."

Then one morning a light came on inside. I realized where I was headed and it was not to Bible study. I found myself deliberately getting up earlier so I could spend more time with my hair and makeup. I wanted to look my best for . . . just a friend? At 7:30 in the morning? Even I couldn't buy that.

I knew I liked being with him. I enjoyed his attention far too much for this to remain a safe place. I was a coward and decided to just disappear. The Bible says it this way: "Joseph fled and got himself out" (Genesis 39:12).

Standing on the brink of adultery is not the time to meet and discuss the situation which is developing. It is not the time to listen to, "But you have to know how I feel. I think of you constantly. You are a craving no one else can satisfy." It is not the time to hear how badly he has it at home and how you cannot possibly take this relationship away, as it is his reason to live.

It *is* the time to get out and get out fast! You will not be strong enough to respond to his seemingly logical appeals and his promises. Get away from the unguarded place.

I did just that. I changed the time I was bringing Amy to school and even came late for a few days, just to be sure I'd miss him. In order to be accountable, I told my husband about the entire situation. I asked the Lord for forgiveness and thanked Him with a grateful heart for opening my eyes in time.

Many women argue, "Men and women can be very close friends without anything going on." Women who say that usually have a man friend they refuse to give up because of an emotional dependency. Emotional intimacy leads to emotional infidelity, and emotional infidelity often leads to physical infidelity.[1]

Do not put yourself in an unguarded place. Satan is ready and waiting to have you take the bait and ruin your life as well as hurt many others.

Your unguarded place may seem innocent enough. Taking my daughter to school was an "okay" place to be. But the timing was wrong! Why? Satan had a trap there.

Your unguarded place may be at work. It could be the doctor's office, the grocery store, even the house you live in. I have a friend who had to move from her present neighborhood because the man next door would not leave her alone. Move, change jobs, change your doctor, take a different route if need be. Just be certain to get out and make it quick!

Unguarded Eyes

We usually think men are the ones stimulated by sight, but many women have told me that a good-looking, well-built male can turn a *woman's* head just as quickly.

The eye is the window to the mind. Whatever we allow to come through will stimulate action of some sort. The first look can trigger an affirming fact, "Yes, he is quite handsome." Taking your eyes away from that sight is wise, because the second look is very likely to say, "Yes, he is handsome and I would just like to enjoy the scenery for a while." This is getting into the danger zone. I call it *The Fatal Distraction*.

David allowed his eyes to wander. He was looking and wanting and eventually was caught in a death trap. David lost his baby son, his dignity, a good friend and the respect of his family. Samson would also have to say "Guilty as charged." He lost his eyesight and eventually his life. Be cautious with your eyes. Do not let them go unguarded.

Trashy magazines and suggestive TV programs can influence you more than you may imagine! Take soap operas—they create a witch who is married to Joe Wonderful. Poor Joe Wonderful falls in love with Sweet Sally who would never treat Joe Wonderful as awful as his witchy wife. Soon you'll be cheering Joe and Sally on, hoping that they'll get together because Joe's situation is so bad. The writers cunningly convince us to go against our standards of morality.

Satan can play that same head game with you: *This man is a much better Christian than your husband. He pays more attention to you and the children than your husband. He treats you so much better, loves you more . . . it must be God's will.* That would *never* be God's voice. His voice doesn't sound like that. His voice sounds like Exodus 20:14: "You shall not commit adultery"; Hosea 3:1: "She was loved by another and is an adulteress"; Matthew 5:27: "Do not commit adultery."

There just isn't any way to justify sin, try as we may. It is sinful to look, lust and love another, except your own husband.

Guard your eyes.

Unguarded Time

"So be careful how you act; these are difficult days. Don't be a fool, be wise" (Ephesians 5:15*a*). David could have used this verse on the day he met Bathsheba. He needed to be wise regarding his unguarded time. One day he found time on his hands: "Not much to do here, with all the other men off fighting a war. Guess I'll take a stroll on the rooftop to see what I can see." If David had been busy, things to do, people to see, a secretary to check with, a boss who was expecting him, some sort of accountability . . . he could not so easily have slept with Bathsheba.

People who have no one to be accountable to are more likely to fall into tempting circumstances. If you are your own boss, your schedule is your own business. You come and go at your leisure. This can be a real liability. Everyone needs to be accountable to someone. You should feel responsible to at least one other person. Why? To keep a check on yourself. You need someone to ask questions concerning your actions.

Being the king, David didn't consider his actions anyone else's business. He felt he could get away with anything. Unguarded time, time when we have complete freedom, can be careless time.

Women may sometimes be left alone at home for weeks at a time. My husband was recently away for two weeks working on his doctorate. A "dear, caring brother" in our congregation gave me a wink and offered to take care of my needs in Richard's absence. I gave him a boot in the behind! Alone times can be unguarded times.

During a loved one's prolonged illness, your vulnerability is at its peak. Exhaustion of body and spirit can weaken your usually strong exterior. All Satan needs is a toehold. Perhaps a soft shoulder to cry on, a caring companion, a strong ship to carry you away from the pain, desolation and emptiness. Be alert to this vulnerable, unguarded time.

Times of great victory can lead us into a euphoric high. Life is great. We feel in control. All is well and unsinkable. I do believe those were the famous last words about the Titanic. Be alert. We are not usually as dependent on the Lord during the afterglow of success. There are many outstanding Christian leaders who are now notches on Satan's belt of immorality. The mighty fall hard. The journey back is long and difficult. Times of great success and mighty victories are key times for Satan to attack.

Kathleen was a successful businesswoman in her late thirties. She was raised in a Christian home and was married to a believer for fifteen years. Three brown-eyed children—little clones of mom and dad—made the family complete.

A few months ago, Kathleen was chosen as one of the top executives in her company. They rewarded her with a business trip to England, a dream come true! The timing wasn't good for her husband and the children's school schedule complicated any possibility of his going along. Kathleen was disappointed but knew Michael had to stay home. Anyway, she would be extremely busy working.

Arriving in England put Kathleen in a dream world. The company made exquisite housing arrangements with a very wealthy client and his wife, who resided just outside of London. The man of the house was tall and dark, and spoke with a British accent. The lady was short and round and had an irritating, squawky voice.

Kathleen found herself promenading all over English soil, enjoying the intoxicating fairy-tale land with little thought of California, the kids or the man to whom she said, "'Till death do us part." The good-looking Englishman caught her at an unguarded time, a time of success and sheer euphoria.

Satan laid the trap shrewdly for Kathleen. She never considered herself vulnerable. After all, she loved her husband and her kids very much. But she paid a high price for the romp in the rustic motherland. Michael found out the hard way from a friend. He left Kathleen alone. She is free to go to England now or anywhere else she chooses.

How sorrowfully she cried to me. She carried so much guilt she could not bear it. Her marriage was ended by her wrong choices during an unguarded high time in her life.

An Unguarded Heart

"Above all else guard your heart, for it is the wellspring of life" (Proverbs 4:23).

The Bible refers to the heart as the core of our very being. In Matthew 15, Jesus reveals that evil comes forth from our heart first. Before action takes place, it is first in our heart. Jeremiah 17:9 warns, "The heart is . . . desperately wicked" (KJV). I think it is fair to say that if we keep our hearts clean and pure before our Lord, we will be able to stay on track.

We must first guard our hearts from *desiring* evil and that will keep our bodies from *doing* evil. How can we keep our hearts from desiring evil? The only way is to be washed daily by the Word of God (Ephesians 5:26). We live in a world of devilish desires, thrills for the moment, temptations, far-out morals, loose living, and media that promote this lifestyle with all their might. Without the Word of God to protect us, we will be reeled in and soon find ourselves in the frying pan.

God knew our hearts would stray. He also knew we needed something to bring them back on track. We face the world alone if we choose to walk out the door without the Word cleansing and guiding us through the day. We unwisely trust our hearts to make good decisions on their own. The Lord must look at us many times and say, "When will you ever learn?"

My family was invited to a friend's home for a Super Bowl Sunday one year. We had a grand day planned: church that morning, then home with our good buddies for a super meal and super fellowship while watching the Super Bowl! The day was going splendidly with a good game and great food. I noticed my young son drooping, so I decided a nap was in order. We marched him to the older boy's room for his slumber. This room was a dream come true for any five-year-old—a number of big, beautiful model planes hung from the ceiling. I laid Aaron down, tucked him in tight and gave him the "don't touch anything" speech.

I returned to the Super Bowl party in the family room, but mindful of my son's inborn curiosity streak, I checked on him and the model airplanes after a few minutes. Aaron was still lying there, eyes as big as chocolate HoHo's, his mind concocting something grand, to be sure. I said, "Aaron, Mommy is going to move you to another bedroom to sleep in. These airplanes are so tempting, I'm afraid you won't be able to resist touching them. I just don't trust you in here, Sugar."

He was thoughtful for a moment, then said, "I trust me!"

We must sound a lot like Aaron at times when we hear the Lord warn us, "Don't go there," "Don't read that," "Stay away from him," or "You can't resist this one; listen to Me." Our words "I trust me!" surely bring sorrow to the Father. He knows we cannot be trusted alone to resist these delicious temptations.

Do not leave your heart unprotected. Satan knows right where to hit. He sees your vulnerable spot and he aims for it. Being in unguarded places, watching with unguarded eyes, spending unguarded time and having unguarded hearts will put us in the dead center of the Garden. The serpent will invite us to eat and we most assuredly will. Do not choose to be somebody's fool, losing everything. Be on guard.

Personal Challenge

1. List in the spaces below areas of your life that might be unguarded today.

     Places:

Time:

Eyes:

Heart:

2. Temptation is no respecter of persons. Write out any tempting situations you have faced.

In the past:

Presently:

3. What should be your plan to avoid these situations?

4. Consider friends or acquaintances who have not fled temptation and found themselves taken in. What was their first mistake? Followed by? How could they have avoided this?

5. Take time now to write a letter to yourself regarding the subject of infidelity. Write as though you were contemplating an affair and this letter is to convince you otherwise. (Use the principles in this chapter and include Scripture.) Seal the letter and open it if you ever find yourself flirting with the idea of immorality.

T · W · E · L · V · E

Baby, "You've Got What It Takes"!

*C*huck and Cindy are a couple who appear happy. They come to church regularly, have a nice home and basically seem to have it all together. They have sweet smiles when out in public. But, as they pull into their driveway at home, the smiles get put away and once again a great gulf of darkness covers their empty hearts.

Cindy is a perfectionist. Her motto: "If you can't do it right, then don't do it at all." She has extremely high goals for herself and demands that she reach those goals, or else! This has proven quite profitable in her career—she has risen to the top of her company in just a few years. Cindy is great at what she does; no one would deny that. But what she puts her family through, especially her husband Chuck, is sheer agony.

Nothing Chuck does is quite up to Cindy's expectations. He feels disapproval from her at all times. When he mows the grass, she surveys the work and finds a spot which needs to be redone. When he buys her a gift, it isn't the right color or the right style, so she returns it to purchase something she can "really use." Rarely can he purchase Cindy a gift of any kind without her being disappointed.

Cindy's same disappointed attitude also comes across in the bedroom. Chuck constantly feels like he is being graded on his performance. Rarely does he feel that he achieves a passing grade. He just can't quite meet her expectations. She wants him to kiss her *here,* but not *there,* and certainly don't do *that!* According to Cindy, there doesn't seem to be any area in which Chuck excels.

Cindy never wanted to push Chuck away. She did love him. But Cindy never learned that "honey attracts, vinegar repels." Chopping and hacking at people is a sure way to devour their self-esteem and diminish their self-worth.

Cindy was far from lighting Chuck's fire. She was fanatically flinging buckets of water on any spark that Chuck might have. Yet, Cindy's deep desire was for her marriage to work.

A few months ago, something happened to Chuck that scared Cindy more than she could express. He began to lose interest in being alone with her. Soon Chuck could not make love to his wife. This was devastating to Cindy. She could not fix this problem, and the doctor could not find any medical reason why this was happening to Chuck.

If you tell someone long enough that they cannot do something, they start to believe it. Chuck's problem was not medical, but a problem related to desire. He had lost the desire to try anymore.

Dr. Paul Pearsall, a sex therapist and director of education at the Kinsey Institute, says, "Problems with desire are the most frequent of sexual problems . . . the number one male sexual problem is the failure to enjoy sex."[1]

Some men are so worried about performance that they lose interest altogether. Sex becomes too stressful. It just isn't fun when it's that much work.

A lot of women start complaining about their husband's lack of interest in sex when they reach mid-life. If the reports we hear from doctors and sex therapists are correct, we wives could help cure this problem.

I do not think we really understand how insecure our husbands are when it comes to their virility, especially when they hit forty. To help them feel secure and successful, we must see ourselves as personal cheerleaders for our husbands. Just how do we go about doing this?

Build Him Up

Although they have a hard time admitting it, men love to be bragged on in one way or another.

Praise is needed in all the little and big things they try. Somewhere I read that for women, sex begins in the kitchen. Perhaps sex begins in the garage or the yard for men.

My husband Richard is usually working on a project of some sort. His latest is restoring a '66 Ford Mustang. I can't tell you the times he has called to me, "Pam, come look at this great-looking carburetor," or he wants to show off the "illustrious interior" he has just completed. I oooh and aaah for a good amount of time, and then return to whatever I was doing before he called me from the sidelines to be cheered on.

I enjoy letting Richard know I'm enthusiastic about his efforts. He's a terrific person and I sincerely think he's deserving of all the cheering I can give him.

And he revels in my praise of whatever he is up to! The yardwork, the way he plays handyman and saves us tons of money (usually), the super job he does delivering his sermon on Sunday, and especially his success on a diet. He waits eagerly to be told, "Losing those extra five pounds, Honey, sure makes you irresistible."

What kind of praise is your lover in need of today?

The following praises come from the Song of Songs. How would your husband feel about some of these compliments, rephrased in today's language?

"Your love is more delightful than wine. Your name is like perfume poured out."

"No wonder the maidens love you!"

"How handsome you are, my lover! Oh, how charming!"

"Your voice is sweet."

"Your face is lovely."

"My heart pounds for you."

"I am faint with love."

"My love is radiant and outstanding among ten thousand."

"His hair is wavy and black as a raven."

"His eyes are like doves."

"His cheeks are like beds of spice."

"His lips are like lilies dripping with myrrh."

"His arms are like rods of gold."

"His body is like polished ivory decorated with sapphires."

"His legs like pillars of marble."

"His mouth is sweetness itself. He is altogether lovely."

"This is my lover, this is my friend."

"Your love burns like blazing fire, like a mighty flame. Many waters cannot quench love; rivers cannot wash it away. If one were to give all the wealth of his house for love, it would be utterly scorned."

After a build-up like that, what man could fail? This woman was sold on her lover, lock, stock and barrel!

Your husband may be far from having the looks of Tom Selleck or the build of Arnold Schwarzennegger, but he can still be your passionate prince, your brave beloved, your exquisite enchanter, your most precious prize.

Major on any and all of the good qualities he has, physically and personally. Concentrate on his positive and not his negative attributes. Dwell on his wonderful ways and be gracious about his flaws and failures.

Practice the power of praising! It will build him up in ways nothing else can.

Be His Queen

If you are a queen, there must be a king of some kind hanging around your castle. With kingship comes authority, and that's a struggle for many women. But take note: Allowing his leadership in your home and life does *not* mean you are asked to be a doormat, or that you are less loved or respected. It means you submit to his authority under the command of the heavenly Father. If you pull one way and your husband another, it not only causes strife between the two of you, but it also forces the children to choose sides.

Kings need honor and respect. Given these, they in turn should be expected to lead in love and fairness. Many kingdoms have found they run most efficiently when king and queen rule together, talking frequently, openly discussing desires, and trying hard to agree together on the business of the kingdom.

Giving Honor

Our friend Mr. Webster says *honor* means, "high respect, distinction given, high rank or position."

Giving your husband honor is biblical. Remember Sarah, Abraham's wife? She called Abraham *lord,* a title of honor in Bible days. I don't think she would call him "my old man" or "the old grouch," "pudgy Pete" or "Harry the hairless." These titles are not endearing—they are endangering. They demean and bring down.

Allowing your husband to lead when it looks like he is headed for the nearest cliff is not easy. A few fleeting warnings discreetly given may put you back on course, but sometimes the king makes a few bumbles in battle before he becomes a great leader. Loyal is the queen who doesn't lead a revolt when this happens. Allow him to learn from mistakes and get things back on track.

Many women make the mistake of always taking over when it looks like a crash and burn is inevitable. Not a good strategy. Sometimes it's only through our failures that we learn the key lessons for future successes.

The chief complaint I hear from women I counsel is, "My husband won't be our spiritual leader." Remember, no one can lead without followers. A leader is motivated by learners, not know-it-alls. Do you intimidate your mate with an "I'm-always-right" attitude? Some women with higher IQs than their husbands continually let them know it! This will never allow a husband to develop his leadership skills. Give him the right and privilege to be the king of his own castle, even if your income makes the castle payments!

On the occasions when your husband is wrong, refrain from correcting him in public. No one likes to be shown up in front of others. Talk to him later in the privacy of your bedroom, making any necessary correction as pain-less as possible.

I hate pain of any kind. Recently I was scheduled for surgery. Everything was set up with the surgeon and anesthesiologist. A few days before I was to go into the hospital, a friend told me of an anesthesiologist who would numb my hand before he put the I.V. needle in. This sounded heavenly to someone who usually gets stuck ten to fifteen times while they search for a good vein!

I immediately made a phone call to the tender, caring doctor who could delete this painful experience from my life. Putting in an I.V. is always far worse for me than the surgery itself. I'm sleeping during the surgery, right?

It was not an easy change to make just two days prior to surgery, but it worked out. It was magnificent! The only way to go as far as I am concerned, because I hate pain.

Sometimes the truth can hurt, like those I.V. need-les. Remember to be merciful, and numb painful truth with a loving spirit as much as you possibly can.

Respect Him

Showing respect is to esteem, honor, and give con-sideration to another's wishes. You give this highest compliment to your husband as you give him reverent respect.

1. *Put your husband first in all human relation-ships.* One common mistake women make is allowing other people and things to come before their husbands. Your husband should come second only to your relationship with Jesus Christ. Putting him first in all human relationships will encourage him to do the same for you. Saying he is first isn't enough. It has to be obvious in deed as well.

If you continually schedule other events when he has time off, it tells him you do not consider spending time alone with him a priority. If you work at home or work part-time, try to be home when he comes home from work. If you are there when he arrives, it says to him, "I have missed you, and I am glad you are home." Greet him with a warm reception and ask how his day has been before telling him about *your* day.

2. *Give your husband equal living space.* Many husbands have only a pitiful little portion of the house they can call their own. His area in the closet is a tiny section while your clothes are spaciously arranged with more than ample room. He must leave his wallet and personal belongings in a cubby hole while you have the entire top of a dresser and night stand.

Mom and the kids have a lot of room to store all their paraphernalia, then they expect Dad to cram his things in cramped quarters. Make room for Daddy! Respect him by giving him adequate space in the castle.

3. *Stand by your husband in front of the children.* From time to time the children will play parent against parent when wanting their way. If the children challenge your husband's decision on a matter, support him even if you think he is wrong. Talk to him about your thoughts when the children are not around. Let him make the apology if need be. The children must not think you are divided, as this allows them to work the two of you against each other.

4. *Don't harp or nag on his faults.* If you've previously talked about a particular shortcoming, don't make it a hobbyhorse, riding it into the ground. Tread in the waters of criticism most carefully or it can be the onset of the second world flood. It is painful to see our own weaknesses. Treat him as you would want him to speak to you about one of your faults.

5. *Give him some privacy.* You certainly should

share intimate time, thoughts and treasures together, but when it comes to personal hygiene, give each other space. Early in my marriage, I was told by an older woman, "Never share a bathroom with your lover. It takes the beauty away from intimacy." I have kept that advice throughout our twenty years of marriage and would encourage you to do the same. In days when we only had one bathroom, we took turns. Now we have a his and hers, and it works out wonderfully.

6. *Do not have lovers' quarrels in public.* Keep your arguments private. When with others, little jabbing remarks at your spouse not only make him embarrassed, but also make those around you uncomfortable. Your belittling actually creates a lot of sympathy for your husband from those listening in. Work things out before you go out in public. I have to admit to cancelling plans with friends several times to work out misunderstandings between Richard and myself.

7. *Learn to enjoy doing something he likes.* My friend Ruth, whose husband loves snow skiing, cannot tolerate the freezing cold that accompanies it. Wanting very much to participate in some type of leisure-time sport with him, she took up golfing. They now enjoy this fun time together.

Find an activity that you can enjoy with your husband. Inquire about his interests. Delight in his dreams. Care about his concerns. Share in his special schemes. Learn to enjoy doing the things that are dear to his heart.

Boldly Affirm

Publicly

Praising your husband publicly will reaffirm to your sweetheart that you believe he is the greatest and you are proud of him. It also makes it clear to others that you are totally satisfied in your marriage and not in the least bit interested in playing any cheating games.

I was paid a high compliment recently. A lady said quite tactfully, "Nobody in their right mind would try anything with you or your husband. You both make it distinctly clear that you are head over heels in love with each other."

I am so glad she noticed. We make a point to publicly say and do things that allow others to see for themselves, "Those two are not available."

If couples would stop being shy about public "I love you's" and handholding, there would be far fewer intrusions into their marriages. Perhaps you would prefer to show your love in a subtle way with phrases like, "I love him when he acts so sentimental," or by just touching each other as you pass, every chance you get. Practice ways of publicly expressing love for one another.

Privately

If you rave about your handsome husband in public, but treat him as if he were infected with something contagious when you are alone, the public gesture means nothing. He will resent those times of public praise and scorn them if you do not treat him with respect during intimate times. He probably will be thinking, "Oh yeah, she's big talk when we're with people, but a cold fish when we get alone."

Margie was one of those big-talk, no-do, wives. When she was alone with her husband Fred, she forgot all about respecting him. Her actions were all show to make people think they were richly romantic in private. But once the audience was out of sight, she became her same cynical self. The public display of affection meant nothing to Fred because privately it was empty, cool indifference.

Private gestures vastly outweigh public gestures. You can't pretend for a long period of time. Eventually the phoniness becomes obvious.

Unable to take this any longer, Fred literally exploded one night at a church party, disclosing all the deceit and disinterest Margie truly possessed. Margie could not believe she had treated Fred in this way. He took her by the arm and led her to the car. Then he began unloading years of resentment he felt toward her.

The three pain-filled hours that followed opened Margie's eyes. She saw that her private responses to Fred had to improve. She had been . . .

. . . pushing him away when he came to her for a loving embrace.

. . . yawning when he was speaking tender words of love.

. . . constantly clock-watching when they did have time together.

. . . frowning at him when he tried something new and exciting.

. . . refusing to give complete attention to him while he was making love to her.

. . . sighing from boredom as he caressed her caringly.

It all said to Fred, "Margie does not respect me like she pretends in public."

Things have worked out for Margie and Fred. She has disciplined herself to be attentive, interested and absorbed in her husband, privately as well as publicly.

Remember to boldly affirm your love and genuine interest in your beloved. Your admiration and respect must be consistent in public and in private.

To be the man you long for him to be, he needs your praise and encouragement. You can help secure your marriage by letting your husband know in every way possible, "You've got what it takes."

Personal Challenge

1. Do you speak words of criticism toward your husband in areas of: work? money? intimacy? gifts to you? If you answered yes to any of these questions, write out your plan for correcting this in your marriage.

2. How can you be more of a cheerleader to your husband? This week, praise him at least three times each day. Try to make this a habit. You can refer to the Song of Solomon for help.

3. Is the king head of your castle? Or is there a power struggle going on? Write out any confession you might have in this area and read or give it to your husband.

4. How do you honor your husband? List those ways. Add new ways in which you could give him honor.

5. Practice a few painless ways you might tell your husband of a certain flaw or weakness he needs to correct.

6. Go over the seven areas of giving respect to your husband found in this chapter. Grade yourself A +, A, B +, B, C +, C, D or F. Be very honest. Then grade yourself again, as you think your husband would grade you. What do your final grades reveal about your respect toward him?

ITEM	How you grade yourself	How your husband would grade you
1. Husband first	_____	_____
2. Equal living space	_____	_____
3. In front of children	_____	_____
4. His faults	_____	_____
5. His privacy	_____	_____
6. Quarrels in public	_____	_____
7. Doing what he likes	_____	_____

7. How can you publicly and privately improve the affirmation of love you have for your husband? Be specific.

T·H·I·R·T·E·E·N

Where Have All the Lovers Gone?

*E*very marriage that is full and rich with love, has withstood many a trial. The sea of matrimony is full of hardships. Understanding this helps us know what to take aboard for the journey:

Love, beyond human understanding.

Fun, to keep the trip from getting boring.

Sex, because it is God's unique way of bonding two people into one. (Aren't you glad He thought of it?)

Respect, so you won't abuse your mate.

Time, the sacred gift you give which helps prove your love.

Unselfishness, because two unselfish people will never get divorced.

I salute you for picking up a book like this. That tells me you want a better marriage than you have right now. All things worth having take a lot of work, will power, and wisdom. I hope this book has shown some wisdom. The work and will power are up to you. If you completed all of the personal challenges, you're well on your way.

Where have all the lovers gone? I trust they are now in each other's arms, to have and to hold, from this day forward, 'til death do us part.

Notes

Chapter 2
1. Quintin Schultze, "Talk About TV," *Moody Monthly* (March 1987), p. 74.
2. J. Allen Petersen, *The Myth of the Greener Grass* (Wheaton, IL: Tyndale House Publishers, Inc., 1983), p. 181.
3. "How Are We Doing?" *Changing Times* (March 1989), p. 28.

Chapter 3
1. J. Allen Petersen, *The Myth of the Greener Grass* (Wheaton, IL: Tyndale House Publishers, Inc., 1983), p. 179.
2. Petersen, p. 51.
3. James Dobson as quoted in *The Myth of the Greener Grass*, p. 51.

Chapter 4
1. "Everyday Life Is Sexier Than You Think, *Glamour* (April 1989), p. 176.
2. Rosemary Ellis, "Sexual Chemistry," *Glamour* (April 1989), p. 322.
3. Tim Stafford, "Sex In and After Eden," *Marriage Partnership* (Summer 1988), p. 107.
4. Michael Metz, "Staying In Love," *Parents* (June 1989), pp. 96-99.
5. Metz, pp. 96-99.
6. Ellis, p. 322.

Chapter 6
1. Billie Sahley and Kathy Birkner, "The Brain, the Body and PMS," *Total Health* (August 1988), pp. 42-44.

Chapter 7
1. Stephanie Young, "Exercise as a Sexual Turn-on," *Glamour* (April 1989).
2. "Concern About Care Should Start in Teenage Years," *Modesto Bee* (August 29, 1989), p. C2.
3. "Beauty Escapes," *Glamour* (April 1989), p. 261.
4. "Victoria Principal's Best Exercises for the Top Five Age-Prone Zones," *Redbook* (October 1988), pp. 120-123.
5. "Controlling Weight," *Modesto Bee* (September 1989).

Chapter 8
1. Much of this chapter is adapted from Florence Littauer's C.L.A.S.S. lecture on the personalities (April 1989) and is used by permission.
2. The "Personality Profile" is reprinted with permission from its author, Fred Littauer.

Chapter 9
1. Maxine Hancock and Karen Mains, *Child Sexual Abuse: A Hope for Healing* (Wheaton, IL: Harold Shaw Publishers, 1987), p. 98.
2. Bob Considine, "Could You Have Loved This Much?" *Guidepost* (March 1959), pp. 182-184.

Chapter 11
1. Andre Bustanoby, "Can Men and Women Be Just Friends?" *Fundamentalist Journal* (September 1986), p. 46.

Chapter 12
1. Paul Pearsall as quoted in "Sex In and After Eden," by Tim Stafford, *Marriage Partnership* (Summer 1988), p. 109.

Making Good
Marriages Better